The Story of the Olympics

Dave Anderson

Foreword by **Carl Lewis**

WILLIAM MORROW AND COMPANY
New York

Permission for photographs is gratefully acknowledged: pages 3, 16, 23, 25, 27, 29, 30, 32, 35, 36, 39, 41, 44, 46, 48, 50, 51, 53, 57, 59, 61, 64, 66, 69, 70, 72, 91, 92, 94, 95, 98, 100, 102, 104, 108, 110, 125, 130, 145, 150—UPI/Bettmann Newsphotos; pages 11, 13, 14—The Bettmann Archive; pages 20, 151—AP/Wide World Photos; pages 74, 78, 79, 80, 82, 86, 113, 117, 121, 122, 126, 136, 139—Reuters/Bettmann Newsphotos; page 133—ALLSPORT USA; page 143—Barton Silverman/New York Times Photos

Printed in the United States of America.

1   2   3   4   5   6   7   8   9   10

Library of Congress Cataloging-in-Publication Data
Anderson, Dave.
The story of the Olympics/Dave Anderson.
p. cm.
Includes index.
Summary: Traces the history of the Olympics from its beginning in 776 B.C. to the present and relates stories of particular events such as track and field, gymnastics, and speed skating.
ISBN 0-688-12954-4
1. Olympics—History—Juvenile literature.
[1. Olympics—History.]   I. Title.
GV721.5.A626 1996   796.48—dc20
95-35067   CIP AC

THE FIRST TIME I KNEW ABOUT THE OLYMPICS was in 1972. I remember watching on television. I was eleven years old and not yet much of an athlete. But both of my parents had competed in track and field and then got into coaching. We were certainly more than casual fans.

Unfortunately, what we all remember most about the 1972 Games in Munich is the terrorists. Of course, being a kid, I understood more about the athletic contests than the tragedy and political implications. But that is really my first memory of the Olympics.

I already knew who Jesse Owens was. I had met him the year before at an age-group meet in Philadelphia. Just knowing he was the winner of four gold medals, as impressive as that was, probably would not have meant too much to me then. But meeting him, hearing my father talk with him about the old days, that is why I came to think so much of Jesse. He was a strong and dedicated person competing in an incredibly difficult era in world history.

Still, it's kind of funny now, in retrospect, when people want to take that little two-minute meeting I had with him as a kid and turn it into something so much bigger than it was. They want to make it like that was the spark for my entire Olympic career or something. No doubt that makes for a nice story, as in creative writing, but not the real story.

Truth is, I would have been crazy to be thinking then about making it to the Olympics. One thing I know for certain: If you had seen me running as a youngster, you never would have guessed I was going to have any chance at all in track and field. Definitely not on the international scene. Definitely not in the Olympics.

I was definitely the runt of the family, small for my age, and my parents figured it would always be that way. We used to have little make-believe track meets out behind our house, and I lost to just about everybody in the neighborhood, even my sister Carol, who was two years younger.

Amazing, though, what can happen when you work hard and keep getting the support of a strong family. I kept growing, kept setting new goals, and the rest, as they say, is history. That is why I always tell young people: Do not ever give up on your dreams. Do not ever let other people tell you what you can or can't achieve. You can achieve whatever you want to. You are the only one who sets the limits.

I have been an Olympian since 1980. Even after all those years, though, I keep learning more and more about the Games. And I like it when I find out something I didn't know. That is why I have found so much enjoyment in what Dave Anderson has done with this book. It is a valuable addition to my Olympic library. And I know you too will get a lot out of it.

Carl Lewis

Contents

part**One**

In the Beginning

To Atlanta from Greece

BEFORE DAWN, HOURS BEFORE THEY HAD TO GO TO work, they gathered in the darkness, waiting for the news. Now, at 7:47 A.M. on September 18, 1990, across the Underground Atlanta plaza, several hundred citizens of Georgia's state capital stared at closed-circuit television screens showing Juan Antonio Samaranch at a lectern in Tokyo, Japan.

"The International Olympic Committee," its president intoned, "has awarded the 1996 Games to..."

Samaranch paused. Atlantans there and in Tokyo held their breath. Athens, the site of the 1896 revival of the Olympics that had originated in Greece in 776 B.C., was hoping to hold the hundredth anniversary modern Olympics, but now Samaranch completed his announcement.

"...Atlanta."

On the plaza in downtown Atlanta people cheered, fireworks exploded, and marching bands tootled. Atlanta, burned by General Sherman's Union troops during the Civil War but now the South's first city, would be the host of the Twenty-sixth Olympic Summer Games. On the fifth round of the International Olympic Committee (IOC) ballot, needing forty-four votes, Atlanta had received fifty-one, Athens thirty-five. But as Atlanta applauded itself, Athens wept.

"Coca-Cola," said Melina Mercouri, referring to Atlanta's most famous product, "won over the Parthenon temple."

Once the minister of culture in Greece and a celebrated actress, Mercouri was a member of the disappointed Greek delegation in Tokyo that had lost to Atlanta's promise of $1.4 billion in revenue.

The romance and spectacle of the Olympics have been upstaged by the reality of the Olympics; both the Summer Games and the Winter Games are now as much big business as they are sport.

The essence of the Olympics still exists. The heritage of the ancient Olympics derived from Olympus, the fabled home of the Greek gods. The romance of an athlete participating rather than winning. The torch relay across nations and continents that leads to the Olympic flame's burning during the sixteen days of competition. The pageantry of the opening and closing ceremonies.

Competitors are inspired by the Olympic motto of *Citius—Altius—Fortius*, words in Latin that translate to, "Faster—Higher—Stronger."

But the Olympics long ago outgrew their roots in Olympia, Greece, where in 776 B.C. in the first recorded ancient Olympics a young Greek named Coroebus won the only event, a race of about two hundred yards, roughly the length of the primitive stadium.

As the first Olympic champion Coroebus was crowned with a wreath woven from the leaves of the olive tree that Hercules, according to the Greek poets, had planted near the Temple of Zeus at Olympia in southwestern Greece.

Originally, the Olympics were a religious experience. Held every four years in an era of almost constant conflict between towns and areas, the Olympics created a truce, a sacred month when athletes and spectators were allowed to travel safely to and from the games. In time the tiered stadium at Olympia held up to fifty thousand people.

By the Thirteenth Olympiad other sports had been added: the discus throw, boxing, wrestling, and chariot racing. Most winners wore their olive wreaths proudly and honestly, but others defied sportsmanship.

In the Ninety-eighth Olympiad, a boxer, Eupolus of Thessaly, was found guilty of bribing three opponents. Over the years several statues atop the Olympic stadium were financed by fines levied on erring athletes.

For years women were forbidden from competing or even attending the Olympics, but eventually women were accepted. At the 128th Olympiad one of the winning chariot drivers was a woman, Belisiche of Macedonia.

When the glory that was Greece eventually dissolved into the grandeur that was Rome, the Olympics changed. Champions demanded money or gifts. Some warring areas no longer observed a truce. Eventually, in A.D. 394, the Olympics were halted by decree of Theodosius I, the Roman emperor. Thirty years later Theodosius II ordered the leveling of the walls around the Olympia enclosure. About a century later earthquakes turned the historic area into ruins, and the rising Alpheus River flowed across what had been the Olympia plains.

Baron Pierre de Coubertin

The Olympics had ceased to exist, but their history endured, especially the lore of the marathon runner.

The marathon as such, now the grueling road race of 26 miles, 385 yards, that is one of the Olympics' signature events and an attraction in so many cities around the world, was not a part of the ancient Olympics, but it evolved from Greek history. When the Greek army routed invading Persians on the plain of Marathon in 490 B.C., a Greek soldier, Pheidippides, a heralded Athenian runner, was ordered to shed his armor and hurry with the news to Athens, about 40 kilometers (25 miles) away. Already weary

from the battle, he puffed along the dusty roads. Staggering into the streets of Athens, his feet cut and bleeding, he yelled, "Rejoice, we conquer!" With a last gasp Pheidippides dropped to the dirt and died.

When the Olympics were revived in 1896, the marathon that Pheidippides had inspired was included in what the Olympics call athletics, what Americans know as track and field. Fourteen centuries after the last of the ancient Olympics, a French promoter of physical education, Baron Pierre de Coubertin, had resurrected the Games.

"The revival of the Olympic Games," Coubertin once said, "will bring athletism to a high state of perfection."

In 1888 the twenty-eight-year-old Coubertin had organized L'Union des Sports Athlétiques to stimulate French interest in sports. The next year he published *La Revue athlétique*, a monthly newspaper. He toured Europe and North America for the French Ministry of Public Instruction. In his travels he visited the ruins at Olympia, excavated by a German archaeological team. In 1859 and again in 1870 the Greeks had tried to revive the Olympics in Athens, without much success.

In 1893 Coubertin invited sportsmen to Paris from all over the world. He announced his plan to revive the Olympics in 1896 in Athens, where George Averoff, a Greek philanthropist, was to provide $360,000 to restore the stadium of Herodis, originally constructed in 330 B.C. On April 6, 1896, exactly 1,502 years after Theodosius I had halted the ancient Olympics, King George I of Greece looked around at the fifty thousand spectators in the new Panathenaic Stadium. "I hereby proclaim," the king said, "the opening of the First International Olympic Games in Athens."

In Atlanta in 1996 the Summer Games will involve some fifteen thousand athletes, coaches, and officials from about two hundred nations competing in about thirty sports, a tribute to the growth and popularity of the Olympics in their centennial celebration. In 1896 in Athens there were only seven sports (track and field, swimming, gymnastics, cycling, fencing, shooting, and tennis) and only eight

The 1896 marathon winner, Spiridon Louis (front row, third from left), sits with Greek and American athletes and officials at Athens.

nations (Greece, Great Britain, France, Germany, Denmark, Hungary, Switzerland, and the United States).

The thirteen Americans did not even constitute an official team; they simply represented themselves. Ten were track-and-field athletes, mostly from the Boston Athletic Association. Two were pistol shooters. One was a swimmer. On their voyage across the Atlantic on a tramp steamer, the *Fulda*, they had exercised on the deck. Most of the European athletes had little regard for these young men from the Western Hemisphere's young nation built by European immigrants.

But one of those Boston athletes, James B. Connolly, won the very first event, known now as the triple jump, then as the hop, step, and jump.

The second event was the discus throw. Bob Garrett, a sturdy Princeton athlete at six-one and 176 pounds, had been practicing with a homemade steel discus before realizing that the Olympic discus was lighter and smaller. He won the discus and later the shot put.

As the first modern Olympics wound down to the marathon on the fifth and final day, the Americans and an Australian runner, Edwin Flack, had won all the track-and-field events.

On the plains near Marathon a Greek army colonel fired a pistol into the air to start twenty-five runners, who included Spiridon Louis, a little Greek shepherd from the Marousi hills. Albin Lermusiaux of France hurried into the lead. The entire route was patrolled by Greek troops, and a squad of Greek cavalry rode with horse-drawn carts behind the runners. Lermusiaux soon was sprawled on one of the carts as a dropout. At the eighteen-mile mark Arthur Blake of England was in front, but as he sagged from exhaustion, the mustached twenty-five-year-old Greek shepherd plodded into the lead. When the runners neared Panathenaic Stadium, a courier informed King George I that Spiridon Louis was ahead. When he wobbled into the stadium, Prince Constantine and Prince George ran alongside him, accompanying him across the finish line as seventy thousand spectators cheered.

Exactly 2,672 years after the ancient Olympics began, Greece had a new Olympic hero. Spiridon Louis had emerged from the pack of marathon runners as the first of the modern Olympic celebrities. An Athens restaurateur offered to feed him; a clothier offered to outfit him; a barber offered to cut his hair for as long as the barber lived. The modern Olympics had begun.

King George I of Greece presents a laurel wreath to Spiridon Louis.

Jim Thorpe and King Gustav

AS THE SS *FINLAND* STEAMED ACROSS THE ATLANTIC toward Stockholm, Sweden, in the summer of 1912, members of the U.S. Olympic team jogged along a specially built cork track. Not far away Jim Thorpe sprawled in a deck chair, his eyes closed.

"I'm practicing the broad jump," he told an inquiring reporter. "I just jumped twenty-three feet, eight inches."

At a muscular six feet and 190 pounds, Thorpe was to compete in both the decathlon and the pentathlon at the Sixth Summer Games, but at twenty-four he was already better known as a football player. When the Carlisle (Pennsylvania) Indian School stunned Harvard, 18–15, the previous season, he produced all its points: four field goals, one touchdown (then worth five points), and one extra point. His track-and-field ability was also awesome. The day of a dual meet Harold Bruce, the Lafayette coach, noticed Glenn ("Pop") Warner, the Carlisle coach, walking with one of his athletes.

"Where's your team?" Bruce asked the Carlisle coach.

Nodding toward Thorpe, Warner said, "Here it is."

Thorpe actually was accompanied by six teammates, not that he needed them. He finished first in the high jump, long jump, shot put, discus, 120-yard high hurdles, and 220-yard low hurdles and third in the 100-yard dash. His teammates combined to take five other events. Carlisle won, 71–41.

The legend of Jim Thorpe was growing. In Stockholm it flourished. In the five-event track-and-field pentathlon, not to be confused with today's military pentathlon, he won the long jump, 200-meter dash, discus, and 1,500-meter run. He finished third in the javelin throw.

Muscles rippling, Jim Thorpe puts the shot at Stockholm.

The ten-event decathlon, still the measure of all-around ability in track and field, began in a hard rain. Thorpe finished a close second in both the 100-meter dash and the long jump, then won the shot put for a leading total of 2,544 points. On the sunny second day he increased his lead by winning the high jump, placing fourth in the 400-meter run, and winning the 110-meter hurdles. On the third day his inexperience cost him victories in the discus, pole vault, and javelin, but he won the 1,500-meter run.

With a total of 8,412.955 points out of a possible 10,000, he had finished nearly 700 points ahead of Hugo Wieslander of Sweden.

During the closing ceremonies later that day King Gustav placed the Olympic laurel wreath on Thorpe's head, draped his pentathlon gold medal around his neck, and presented him with a huge bronze bust of his own royal likeness. Thorpe returned later for another wreath, his decathlon gold medal, and a jeweled silver miniature Viking ship. King Gustav shook hands and said, "You, sir, are the greatest athlete in the world."

Somewhat embarrassed, somewhat awkward, the greatest athlete in the world said, "Thanks, King."

Jim Thorpe had put the Olympics on the world map. In those years, long before radio and television, the accomplishments of American athletes in the five previous Olympics since 1896 had been buried, if not ignored, by many American newspapers. No longer. Thorpe created page-one headlines. When he returned to Carlisle, he added to the legend. In a 27–6 football victory over Army, he accounted for all his team's points: three field goals, two touchdowns, a touchdown pass, and three extra points. With the Canton Bulldogs he was to earn a Pro Football Hall of Fame plaque. He also was a major-league baseball outfielder for six seasons, mostly with the New York Giants.

When the Associated Press polled American sportswriters in 1950 to select the Athlete of the Half Century, Thorpe won in a landslide.

Sadly, in 1913 Thorpe was stripped of his Olympic gold medals and trophies after he acknowledged having received about sixty dollars a month to play semipro baseball in North Carolina in 1908 and 1909. Although common among collegians then, the practice violated the era's Olympic code forbidding an athlete from competing if he or she had been paid to play a sport, even if it was different from his or her Olympic sport. Instead of adopting a fictitious name, as others had, Thorpe had played under his real name, a naive mistake.

Eventually, in 1982, twenty-nine years after Thorpe's death and badgered by Charlotte Thorpe's campaign on behalf of her father, the IOC agreed to replace his Olympic gold medals.

Jim Thorpe remains arguably the best athlete in American history. His versatility in the Olympics, pro football, and major-league baseball has never been matched. Although many Olympic decathletes have surpassed Thorpe's decathlon point totals, track-and-field experts wonder what he might have been able to accomplish using today's sophisticated training methods.

But the 1912 Olympics in Stockholm is also remembered for Europe's celebrating an idol, Hannes Kolehmainen, the first of the Flying Finn distance runners. He won gold medals at 5,000 meters and 10,000 meters and in the cross-country race. Twenty-eight nations sent twenty-five hundred athletes, including fifty-seven women competing in swimming and diving for the first time. At last the Olympics had emerged as a spectacle after nearly two decades of struggle since the 1896 revival.

Sunday Afternoon in Paris

In 1900 the second modern Olympics were unofficially attached to the Paris Exposition as "international championships." In the tree-shaded Bois de Boulogne runners competed on a five-hundred-meter oval across a bumpy grass field. When the unofficial U.S. team learned that the French hosts had changed the schedule to put the second day of competition on Sunday instead of Monday, it protested. Blue laws in many American cities then prohibited Sunday baseball and college sports.

"Everybody here feels it is a most contemptible trick," said Amos Alonzo Stagg, the famous football coach who was managing the University of Chicago team. "Not a single university would have sent a team had it not been definitely announced that the games would not be held on a Sunday."

Some of the Americans agreed to compete on Sunday; some didn't. It didn't make much difference. In the twenty-three track-and-field events, four Americans (Alvin Kraenzlein, Ray Ewry, Irving Baxter, and John Walter Tewksbury) combined for eleven firsts, five seconds, and one third. Kraenzlein, a twenty-three-year-old Penn graduate, won the 60-meter dash, the 110-meter high hurdles, the 200-meter low hurdles, and the long jump. He is the only athlete ever to win four individual track-and-field events in the same Olympics. Two team sports, soccer and water polo, also were introduced in Paris.

Women weren't allowed to compete in Olympic track and field until 1928 and in basketball until 1976, but the first two women Olympic champions emerged in Paris in 1900: Peggy Abbott in golf, Charlotte Cooper in tennis.

Abbott, a member of the Chicago Golf Club, happened to be in France on vacation with her mother. The first U.S. female to win a gold medal, she took the nine-hole event with a score of 47, the only time the Olympics included women's golf. Cooper, the women's tennis champion, was from Great Britain.

The Song for St. Louis

In 1904 at St. Louis the Olympics again were part of an international festival, the Louisiana Purchase Exposition, known as the St. Louis World's Fair. "Meet me in St. Louis, Louis," a popular song suggested. "Meet me at the fair."

Teams from Germany, Ireland, Greece, Hungary, Cuba, Canada, and Australia met at the fair, but British and French athletes stayed away. So did Yale and Penn college athletes. In the first Olympics to include boxing and wrestling, American athletes won seventy-seven events. But with St. Louis not having attracted many European nations to America's then remote Midwest, Greece offered to be the permanent host.

Baron de Coubertin suggested a compromise: Starting in 1906, and every four years after that, unofficial mid-Olympics would be held in Athens to stir Olympic interest. The 1906 mid-Olympics took place, but internal problems prompted the Greeks to cancel the 1910 competition.

The concept of a regularly scheduled mid-Olympics was dead,

although the 1906 Games have endured as official. And for the United States the significance of the 1906 mid-Olympics remains. The athletes represented the first official U.S. team, as selected by a national Olympic committee (headed by an honorary chairman, President Theodore Roosevelt) and financed by nationwide contributions to a special Olympic fund. They were the first Games in which U.S. athletes wore official uniforms and the first to produce a virtual unknown as an Olympic hero, Paul Pilgrim.

"We're in good financial shape," James E. Sullivan of the U.S. Olympic Committee told Matt Halpin, the New York Athletic Club official who managed the American team. "You can add any one man you want to the squad."

Halpin chose the twenty-year-old Pilgrim, a NYAC middle-distance runner. Pilgrim paid his own way for the American team's

Paul Pilgrim wins the 800 gold at Athens.

trip on the SS *Barbarossa* from New York to Naples, a train across Italy, another ship to Greece, then a train to Athens and the Panathenaic Stadium's clockwise track, where he quietly qualified for the 400-meter final.

"That's wonderful, Paul," Halpin said. "Now nobody can criticize us for you being here."

During the Atlantic voyage Harry Hillman, the American who had won the Olympic 400 in St. Louis, had suffered a bruised knee when a huge wave splashed across the deck. Wyndham Halswelle, a British Army lieutenant, was now the favorite. Halswelle turned into the stretch with the lead, but Pilgrim sprinted past him for the gold medal. In the 800-meter final the next day Jim Lightbody, the American who had won the event in St. Louis, appeared in command until Pilgrim sprinted past him for a victorious double.

The Battle of Shepherd's Bush

The 1908 Olympics in London, the first in which gold, silver, and bronze medals were awarded, are remembered as the Battle of Shepherd's Bush for the furors in that area of the British capital. When no American flag was on display during the opening ceremony, several U.S. athletes waved small American flags as they marched into the Olympic Stadium after each nation had dipped its flag in tribute to King Edward VII. But the U.S. flag bearer, weight thrower Martin Sheridan, strode past the king's box without lowering the Stars and Stripes.

"This flag," Sheridan barked later, "dips to no earthly king."

In the opening 400-meter run two Americans, John Carpenter of Cornell and William Robbins of Harvard, appeared about to finish one, two when British officials hurried onto the track, shouting, "Foul! Foul!" One judge grabbed another American runner, John Taylor; another judge cut the tape before Carpenter, Robbins, and Wyndham Halswelle of Great Britain finished in that order. The judges huddled, disqualified Carpenter for interfering with

Halswelle, and ordered the other three to rerun the race. James E. Sullivan, the respected American official, was enraged.

"Never in my life," he growled, "and I have been attending athletic meetings for thirty-one years, have I witnessed a scene that struck me as being so unsportsmanlike and unfair. The race was as fair as any race ever run."

When U.S. officials withdrew both Robbins and Taylor from the rerun in protest, Halswelle won the gold medal in the only walkover in Olympic history.

The marathon provided another controversy. To allow King Edward's grandchildren to watch the start, the course began in front of Windsor Castle and ended in Shepherd's Bush stadium, exactly 26 miles, 385 yards (42.195 kilometers) away—the marathon distance ever since. Dorando Pietri of Italy arrived in the stadium first but wobbled the wrong way and collapsed. Officials helped Pietri to his feet and dragged him across the finish line thirty-eight seconds before Johnny Hayes, a 126-pound New Yorker, trotted home unaided.

British officials quickly raised the Italian flag for Pietri, but Hayes later was awarded the gold medal, prompting the Italian contingent to argue that Pietri would have been able to finish first even if the British officials hadn't helped him. The controversies created a rule for future Olympics: The judges would be from various nations, not only from the host nation.

Ray Ewry emerged as a legendary Olympian, winning a total of ten events from 1900 to 1908 while dominating the standing high jump and the standing long jump for nearly a decade. As a frail youngster in Lafayette, Indiana, he had turned to sports after a polio attack. Known as Deac, he earned a mechanical engineering degree at Purdue before working in New York as a hydraulic engineer. His records remain unbroken because after 1912 the Olympics eliminated the standing high jump and the standing long jump.

But more than any other early champion Jim Thorpe turned the world spotlight on the Olympics as a world stage. Just in time. Two

Ray Ewry leaped to a record ten gold medals.

years before the scheduled 1916 Games in Berlin, a Bosnian Serb, nineteen-year-old Gavrilo Princip, assassinated Archduke Franz Ferdinand, the heir to the Austro-Hungarian throne. The shooting occurred in Sarajevo, the city that staged the 1984 Winter Games only to be ravaged less than a decade later in Yugoslavia's civil war.

The assassination provoked World War I, which canceled the 1916 Games, but the Olympics were now sturdy enough to survive.

The Babe and Tarzan

AS A TEENAGER SHE WASN'T A BIG GIRL, ABOUT FIVE-four and a lean 110 pounds, but Mildred ("Babe") Didrikson was a natural athlete. The sixth of seven children of immigrant Norwegian parents, she had grown up in Beaumont, Texas, playing with her brothers and sisters and all the other neighborhood youngsters.

"We played baseball and football with the boys," she once said, "but the boys hated to see us show up when they were playing football. That meant they'd have to stop tackling and switch to touch tag."

Her father, Ole, a cabinetmaker when he wasn't a seaman, had created a homemade gymnasium for his kids. In the backyard of their small home he put up bars for jumping. In the garage he devised a homemade barbell for weight lifting—a broomstick with a flat iron attached to each end.

"He put it there for the boys," the Babe recalled, "but my sister Lillie and I would get in there and work out with it too."

That broomstick with a flat iron at each end deserves to be on display in the Olympic museum in Lausanne, Switzerland, along with the films, photos, and newspaper accounts of what eighteen-year-old Babe Didrikson accomplished in women's track and field at the 1932 Summer Games in the Los Angeles Coliseum.

On the first day she won the gold medal in the javelin while setting a world record with a throw of 143 feet, 4 inches.

On the fifth day she won the gold medal in the 80-meter hurdles while setting a world record with a time of 11.7 seconds.

On the sixth day she and American teammate Jean Shiley shared a world record in the high jump with a leap of 5 feet, 5 inches.

Babe Didrikson set a world record in the javelin at Los Angeles.

But when her last jump-off was ruled invalid because she dived headfirst over the bar instead of feetfirst, she was placed second and awarded the silver medal. In later years that headfirst style, known as the western roll, was permitted. But even with her disqualification in the high jump she had set three world records.

"I'd break 'em all," she said, meaning world records, "if they'd let me."

Under Olympic rules then a woman was allowed to enter only three track-and-field events, because officials questioned female stamina; that probably deprived the Babe of more medals. According to Grantland Rice, the premier sports columnist of that time, she was "the most flawless section of muscle harmony, of complete mental and physical coordination the world of sport has ever known." But the Babe's boasting annoyed some of her Olympic teammates. Upon meeting Helene Madison, a swimmer who won three gold medals at Los Angeles, she asked how fast Madison could swim the 100-meter freestyle. When Madison told her, the Babe laughed.

"Shucks, lady," she said. "I can beat that by three seconds just practicin'."

Considering the Babe's athletic ability, maybe she could have bettered Madison's time. This was a wonderwoman, as she had proved a month earlier in the women's National Amateur Athletic Union championships. The only member of the Employers Casualty Insurance team in Dallas, she won the javelin, shot put, long jump, 80-meter hurdles, and baseball throw, tied for first in the high jump, and was fourth in the discus.

With her thirty points she won the team title all by herself; the Illinois Women's Athletic Club, with twenty-two competitors, was a distant second with twenty-two points.

But for the Babe, track and field had been an afterthought. She had joined Employers Casualty in 1930 as a sixteen-year-old basketball player who had been all-city and all-state at Beaumont High. In the women's national amateur basketball tournament during those years before many colleges sponsored women's sports, she was the equivalent of an All-America three years in a row.

"Is there anything you don't play?" she was asked.

"Yeah," she replied with a quick smile. "Dolls."

After the Olympics the Babe turned to golf. Married in 1938 to wrestler George Zaharias, she won the 1946 U.S. Women's Amateur and the 1947 British Women's Amateur (the first American to do so). She later won the U.S. Women's Open three times, including a twelve-stroke triumph in 1954 after requiring surgery for cancer, the disease she died from in 1956.

Just as Jim Thorpe was hailed as the Athlete of the Half Century in 1950 by the Associated Press, Babe Didrikson Zaharias was voted the Female Athlete of the Half Century.

The Olympics had been the Babe's first world stage, but she shared it with another American woman. Stanislawa Walasiewicz, better known as Stella Walsh, set a world record in the 100-meter sprint. Over more than two decades she won thirty-five national titles in the sprints, long jump, and discus, another wonderwoman in an era when females seldom were recognized for their athletic accomplishments.

At Los Angeles the 121 women athletes stayed in hotels apart from the first Olympic Village, where nearly 1,300 male athletes from thirty-nine nations were lodged in newly built cottages and apartments with dining rooms and a social hall.

Stella Walsh snaps the tape in the 100 at Los Angeles.

Mutiny at Antwerp

Twelve years earlier in Antwerp, Belgium, the preparations had been minimal. Antwerp had less than a year to get ready for the 1920 Summer Games after the November 11, 1918, armistice finally ended World War I.

When the U.S. athletes arrived on an old army transport ship, the *Princess Matoika*, they were consigned to an empty schoolhouse that resembled a military barracks. After two days of sleeping on cots and eating unappetizing food, hop-step-and-jumper Dan Ahearn moved elsewhere without permission from the U.S. officials.

Ahearn was suspended, but two hundred American athletes signed a petition demanding his reinstatement, along with better food and lodging. Otherwise they would not compete.

"You can't do that," Barton S. Weeks of the U.S. Olympic Committee (USOC) told the rebels. "You can't betray the people who sent you over here. You must carry on. The committee must carry on. What would you do if the committee quit?"

"Get a better one," one athlete yelled.

The lodging didn't improve, but Ahearn was reinstated, and the athletes competed as the first Olympic flag fluttered in the Belgian breezes. Its five circles represented the five major continents: Europe, Asia, Africa, North America, and South America. At least one of the colors of the five rings (red, blue, yellow, green, and black) is found in the flag of every nation in the world. At the opening ceremony the athletes took the Olympic oath for the first time.

"In the name of all competitors," they repeated, "I swear that I will take part in the Olympic Games respecting and abiding by the rules which govern them, in the true spirit of sportsmanship, for the glory of sport and the honor of our country."

Of the American athletes, Charley Paddock reigned as the "world's fastest human" in the 100-meter dash. But the name to emerge from these Olympics was that of barrel-chested Paavo Nurmi, who grew up in Turku, Finland, running alongside the morning mail train and often beating it to the next town. He had a slow heartbeat, only forty beats a minute. He ran with no emotion, glancing every so often at a stopwatch on his left wrist. And he supposedly had a different diet.

"Did you eat black bread and fish today?" he once was asked.

"No black bread and fish any day," he replied with a shrug.

Nurmi's favorite food was oatmeal. After he finished second in the 5,000-meter run to Joseph Guillemot, who had been gassed as a French soldier during the war, Nurmi won the 10,000 and the 10,000 cross-country races. Including the 1924 and 1928 Olympics, he was to win seven gold medals and three silver medals. Over the next decade he held world records in twelve events: the 1,500, 2,000, 3,000, 5,000, 10,000, and 20,000 meters as well as one mile, two miles, three miles, four miles, five miles, and six miles.

"He's a mechanical Frankenstein," one sportswriter observed, "created to annihilate time."

Breathing easily, Paavo Nurmi crosses the 1,500 finish line at Paris.

The Return to Paris

In 1924 at Paris no mutiny over living conditions was necessary. The U.S. team stayed at Rocquencourt, once the estate of one of Napoleon's marshals. The athletes checked into eleven new concrete

Johnny Weissmuller at Paris in 1924, before he became "Tarzan"

barracks while the officials were quartered in the château itself. They had docked at Cherbourg after a pleasant voyage on the *America*, equipped with a cork track, boxing rings, wrestling mats, and a canvas swimming tank from which handsome, husky Johnny Weissmuller emerged as the Olympics' first Hollywood star. He won the 100 freestyle and the 400 freestyle and swam on the winning 4 x 200 freestyle relay, an event that had been included in the Olympic swimming program in 1908 in order to add a team concept.

At the 1928 Summer Games in Amsterdam, Holland, the first in which women competed in track and field, Elizabeth Robinson won the 100, and Ray Barbuti, a Syracuse University football player, took the 400 and anchored the 4 x 400 relay, but Weissmuller remained America's idol.

"Even as a kid I never tensed up," he said. "Not even the Olympics bothered me."

Weissmuller, who represented the Illinois Athletic Club, was to set world records in sixty-seven different swimming events, from

50 yards (swimming's equivalent of a 200-meter sprint) to 880 yards (the equivalent of a 2-mile run).

"Johnny didn't care what the event was," his coach, Bill Bachrach, said, "just as long as they had a tank, timers, and a finish line."

At a muscular six-three and 190 pounds, Weissmuller was later seen by motion-picture audiences worldwide, swinging from vines as Tarzan for two decades.

Unlike the 1900 fiasco in Paris, the 1924 Olympics there were a smashing success. Crowds of up to sixty thousand filled Colombes Stadium daily. Some three thousand athletes from forty-four nations attended, notably Harold Abrahams, a cigar-smoking, ale-drinking British sprinter whose gold medal in the 100 was chronicled more than half a century later in an award-winning motion picture, *Chariots of Fire*. Another competitor that year was Benjamin Spock, an American rower whose medical advice for children was heeded decades later.

The Olympics on Ice and Snow

Six months earlier the first Winter Games had been staged at Chamonix, snuggled in the French Alps near the Swiss and Italian borders. The requirement for a winter sport, then and now, is that the competition be held on ice or snow.

Those first Winter Games had five sports: ice hockey, figure skating, speed skating, cross-country skiing, and ski jumping. In the ice hockey tournament Canada, where British soldiers had originated the game on frozen Ontario ponds, outscored five teams, 110–3, including a 6–1 victory over the United States in the final. Figure skating for both men and women had been part of the Summer Games in 1908, 1912, and 1920, but now it was center stage in the Winter Games. In the 1924 women's figure skating competition Sonja Henie, an eleven-year-old Norwegian, finished last. But in each of the next three Winter Olympics, beginning at St. Moritz, Switzerland, in 1928, the tiny blonde soared to the gold medal.

With a smile for Hollywood, Sonja Henie floats to her 1936 gold medal.

"Most always I win," she enjoyed saying.

Sonja Henie had been the Norwegian champion at eleven, but after her last-place finish at Chamonix, she studied the ballerina Anna Pavlova and practiced seven hours a day under the coaching of her father, Wilhelm, an Oslo shopkeeper who had been a European cyclist. Beginning in 1927, Henie won ten consecutive world championships.

After her third Olympic gold medal at Garmisch-Partenkirchen, Germany, in 1936, the five-two, 90-pound skater signed a Hollywood contract and starred in several motion pictures, emerging in 1939 as the number-three box-office attraction, behind Shirley Temple and Clark Gable. She earned millions, much of it from starring in her own touring ice show.

In 1932 the Winter Games took place in Lake Placid, New York, an Adirondack mountain village. Three hundred athletes from seventeen nations attended these first Winter Games to be held in the United States, and two American speed skaters, Irving Jaffee and Jack Shea, each earned two gold medals. Billy Fiske repeated his 1928 triumph as the driver of the winning four-man bobsled that included Eddie Eagan, a boxer in 1920 and the only athlete to win a gold medal in both the Summer and Winter Games.

Six months later America basked in Babe Didrikson's triumphs at Los Angeles. At the conclusion of these Games the 1936 Summer Olympics were awarded to Berlin, Germany, long before the IOC leaders and the world realized that Adolf Hitler would be turning his Nazi soldiers toward World War II.

Jesse Owens and Hitler

AS THE FIRST OLYMPIC TORCH RELAY LIGHTED THE roads from Olympia, Greece, through seven European nations to Berlin, as more than five thousand athletes from fifty-three nations gathered there for the 1936 Summer Games, much of the world was in turmoil, if not in flames. Italy had conquered Ethiopia. Japan had invaded Manchuria. Greece and Austria were seething. Britain and France were objecting to the German zeppelin, the *Hindenburg*, floating in the sky above their military installations. Spain was about to erupt in civil war.

In Germany itself Hitler's storm troopers had begun to persecute Jews, decreed as inferior to the "Aryan" race. In time blacks also would be targeted by Nazi soldiers.

During the opening ceremony in the sparkling new thirty-million-dollar Olympic Stadium, athletes from countries friendly to Hitler's philosophy used the Nazi salute as they passed his box. When the U.S. team marched in, many of the 110,000 spectators whistled, the European version of booing. Among the American athletes were ten blacks, notably James Cleveland ("Jesse") Owens, an Ohio State sprinter and long jumper.

At the 1935 Big Ten championships Owens, a sophomore from Cleveland, had set world records in the 220-yard dash, the 220-yard low hurdles, and the long jump. He had also tied the world record in the 100-yard dash. All within two hours.

"In the sprints, I stick with the field, breathing naturally until thirty yards from the finish," he explained. "Then I take one big breath, hold it, tense all my abdominal muscles and set sail. I do the

Strides ahead of his competitors, Jesse Owens streaks to the 200 gold at Berlin.

same thing in the jump. About thirteen yards from the takeoff, I get that big breath and then I don't let it out until I'm safely in the pits."

In the 1936 Summer Games this seventh child of a poor Alabama cotton picker, this grandson of slaves, projected the black athlete onto the Olympic stage and embarrassed Hitler.

When a German shot putter, Hans Woellke, won the first track-and-field event, Hitler congratulated him, just as he had congratulated Sonja Henie at the Winter Games in Garmisch-Partenkirchen, Germany, six months earlier. But when two members of what the official Nazi newspaper *Der Angriff* described as America's "black auxiliaries," Cornelius Johnson and Dave Albritton, finished one, two in the high jump, Hitler suddenly left his box.

Some people insisted that Hitler had snubbed the black Americans. Others insisted that he had learned that Olympic protocol prohibited the leader of the host nation from offering congratulations publicly to any athlete.

The next day Owens darted to the gold medal in the 100 in 10.3 seconds, and another American black, Ralph Metcalfe, took the silver. Hitler had gone under the stands earlier to congratulate two German hammer throwers, Karl Hein and Erwin Blask, for finishing first and second. But after Owens's victory Hitler was nowhere to be seen.

On the third day Owens glided through his 200-meter heat, then moved to the long jump pit. On his first qualifying attempt an official waved a red flag. Owens had been wearing his sweatsuit top. On his second attempt, another red flag. An official ruled that Owens had fouled, stepping just beyond the takeoff line before jumping.

Another foul and Owens would be disqualified. But now, awaiting his third and final jump, he heard a German voice say, "I'm Lutz Long. I don't think we've met."

Owens turned and said, "Glad to meet you."

The German long jumper, the leading qualifier, had a suggestion for the American who was the world-record holder. "You should be

Jesse Owens (center) salutes the American flag from the long-jump medal platform with Germany's Lutz Long (right), Japan's Naoto Tajima (left), and Olympic officials.

able to qualify with your eyes closed," Long said. "Why don't you draw a line a few inches in back of the takeoff line and aim your takeoff from there? You'll be sure not to foul. And you certainly ought to jump far enough to qualify."

Owens thanked Long, then drew a small line at least a foot behind the takeoff line. On his final jump he soared more than a foot beyond the 23-foot, 5½-inch qualifying distance. He later won the gold medal with an Olympic-record 26 feet, 5⁵⁄₁₆ inches.

"The instant I landed," Owens said later, "Lutz Long was at my side, congratulating me. And it wasn't a fake smile. It took a lot of courage for him to befriend me in front of Hitler."

Surrounded by storm troopers, Hitler hurried under the stands to congratulate Long for earning the silver medal. Maybe the Führer didn't realize how Long's kindness had helped Owens qualify after two fouls. Long later was killed while serving in the German army during World War II.

On the fourth day Owens won the 200-meter dash in a world-record 20.7 seconds, but just after he flashed across the finish line, a heavy rain began. By the time Owens was awarded his gold medal, an olive wreath, and a little oak sapling in a pot, Hitler had left the stadium.

On the eighth day Owens earned his fourth gold medal, running the opening leg on the 400-meter relay team's victory that aroused an American controversy.

In putting Owens and Metcalfe on the relay at the last minute to run with Foy Draper and Frank Wykoff, Coach Lawson Robertson dropped two Jewish sprinters, Marty Glickman (later a New York sportscaster) and Sam Stoller. Some observers assumed that Hitler's anti-Semitism had influenced Robertson, but the coach's explanation was that he feared the Italian and German relay teams. Robertson also had substituted two blacks for the two Jewish sprinters, hardly a bow to Nazi philosophy.

"Owens and Metcalfe are our two best sprinters," the coach said. "Our relay team is better with them on it."

With Owens and Metcalfe bursting through the first two legs, the U.S. team set a world record of 39.3 seconds. In all, four blacks (Owens, high jumper Johnson, 400 champion Archie Williams, and 800 champion John Woodruff) won six of the eleven individual gold medals earned by American track-and-field athletes. Including the 400 relay victory, the U.S. team had twelve golds in track and field, one more than all the other nations combined. Not that Owens was disappointed at Hitler's snub.

"It was all right," he said later. "I didn't go over to Germany to shake hands with Hitler anyway."

Owens almost hadn't gone to Germany at all. Not long after Hitler emerged as Germany's leader, many Americans argued that if the United States sent an Olympic team to Berlin, it would provide tacit approval for Hitler's tyrannical dictatorship, especially his anti-Semitic philosophy. But the USOC president, Avery Brundage, a Chicago hotel owner who had been a decathlon teammate of Jim Thorpe in 1912, argued against a boycott.

"I don't think we have any business to meddle in this question," Brundage said. "We are a sports group, organized and pledged to promote clean competition and sportsmanship. When we let politics, racial questions, religious or social disputes creep into our actions, we're in for trouble."

Considering how Hitler later ravaged Europe, what Brundage considered "trouble" turned out to be minimal. But these were the first Olympics to be used as a national spectacle, the first to project a political philosophy. Hitler was shrewd enough to put Germany's best foot forward during the Olympics, even if that booted foot did a goose step. All the anti-Semitic signs in Berlin had been taken down. All the houses facing the Olympic venues had been painted or cleaned and their window boxes filled with flowers. New brick and stucco cottages had been erected in a sprawling Olympic Village that housed 3,741 athletes from forty-nine nations.

At the opening ceremony Spiridon Louis, the winner of the 1896

Olympic marathon in Athens, presented Hitler with an olive branch from Olympia itself. And the IOC awarded the 1940 Summer Games to Tokyo, Japan.

But in 1939, his Olympic showcase forgotten, Hitler ordered his army to roll into Poland in a blitzkrieg, the beginning of the Nazi takeover of most of Europe. After Germany and Japan surrendered in 1945, ending World War II, the IOC designated bomb-battered London as the 1948 site.

London's Teenage Theater

Peace after nearly a decade of war prompted fifty-nine nations to send 4,468 athletes in twenty-five sports to London, where the British, without the money or the materials to construct an Olympic Village, lodged the men at an army camp in Uxbridge, the women in the Southlands College dorms.

Four months earlier one of the Americans staying in an Uxbridge barracks had never held a javelin, never pole-vaulted, never run a 1,500, and rarely competed in the 100, 400, or long jump. Primarily a running back in football and a high-scoring basketball player at Tulare (California) High School, seventeen-year-old Bob Mathias had concentrated on the hurdles, high jump, and discus during the track-and-field season.

"I wish you'd try the decathlon," his coach, Virgil Jackson, suggested. "You'd be a cinch to make the Olympic team in 1952."

At seventeen, Bob Mathias whirls the discus in the London mud.

Within a month Mathias, husky at six-two and 190 pounds, had won the ten-event decathlon in a meet with several college athletes. Two weeks later he won the U.S. decathlon title, thereby qualifying for the Olympic team. But after the 100 and 400 in Wembley Stadium, he was in jeopardy. He not only was trailing Enrique Kistenmacher, an Argentine army officer, and Ignace Heinrich of France but twice had failed at 5-9 in the high jump when he knew he needed to clear 6 feet if he was to stay in contention.

"Forget about form," he mumbled to himself as he awaited his final jump. "Just get over the bar."

He did. He eventually cleared 6 feet, 1¼ inches. But after the shot put and the high jump, he was still third. The next morning he awoke early and ate a steak for breakfast. After the 110-meter hurdles and the discus, he was in first place, but now a cold, raw rain was falling as darkness was descending. Between his events he huddled in a blanket and munched on a box lunch. On his first vault the bar was a blur as he hurried down the slippery runway holding a rain-slicked pole. After he stepped beyond the foul line on his first javelin throw, officials shone flashlights on it. About an hour before midnight, after more than twelve hours of competition, he completed the 1,500 to assure his gold medal.

"I never worked so long and so hard for anything in my life," Mathias said. "I wouldn't do this again for a million dollars."

Four years later in Helsinki at age twenty-one, Bob Mathias did it again, winning another decathlon gold medal and setting a world record. He was to go on to play fullback at Stanford, act in motion pictures, and represent the Tulare district in the House of Representatives.

Two other Americans—Harrison Dillard, normally a hurdler, and Mel Patton—won gold medals in London in the 100 and 200, respectively.

But to many observers the most remarkable athlete of the 1948 Olympics was a twenty-eight-year-old mother of two. As a Dutch

In the rain, Fanny Blankers-Koen (right) streaks to the 200 gold at London.

teenager Fanny Blankers-Koen had finished sixth in the high jump at Berlin before surviving the Nazi occupation. Now, twelve years later, she won the women's 100, 200, and 80-meter hurdles, and she anchored the winning 4 x 100-meter relay team. She might have won six gold medals had she been able to enter the high jump and the long jump; she held the world record in both. But like Babe Didrikson in 1932, she was limited to three individual events.

Throughout the 1948 Olympics several middle-aged men in dark suits sat quietly at the various venues, intently studying the athletes, taking notes, snapping pictures. They were Soviet coaches and trainers.

In 1947 the Soviet Union, its army having driven Hitler's troops out of Poland and Czechoslovakia while the Allies were liberating

Western Europe, had been recognized as an Olympic nation. But the Soviet sports leaders chose not to send teams to London or to St. Moritz, site of the 1948 Winter Games, where figure-skater Dick Button and slalom skier Gretchen Fraser won America's first gold medals in those sports. Instead the Soviet observers were preparing for 1952.

The Russians were coming.

The Soviet Invasion

DAY BY DAY THE 1952 SUMMER GAMES IN HELSINKI, Finland, were turning into a duel not only between the athletes from the United States and the Soviet Union but also between the ideologies of capitalism and communism. In the years after World War II the Soviet leaders had erected what British Prime Minister Winston Churchill called an Iron Curtain to separate its Communist-bloc nations in Eastern Europe from the free world. Now, with the Soviets finally competing in the Olympics, unofficial team points were upstaging individual accomplishments.

In the team standings, points were awarded to nations on the basis of ten points for a first-place finish, five for second, four for third, three for fourth, two for fifth, and one for sixth.

"If this becomes a great contest between the great nations rich in talent and resources," warned Avery Brundage, the IOC president, "the spirit of the Olympics will be destroyed."

That spirit had already been wounded. While spurning the Winter Games in Oslo, Norway, earlier in the year, the Soviets had spent millions on preparing athletes for the Summer Games in Helsinki, Finland, just across the border separating the two nations. According to the Olympic code, participating was the essence of the Games, but the Soviets were there to win.

"Sports," proclaimed Pjotr Sobolev, secretary-general of the Soviet Olympic Committee, "will be a weapon in the fight for peace and the promotion of friendship among all peoples."

To Olympic officials, the Soviets' idea of friendship was suspect. The direct route for the torch relay from Olympia to Helsinki wound

Prepared and precise, the Soviet Union's first Olympic team marches into Helsinki's opening ceremony.

through the Soviet Union, but the Soviets refused to cooperate, forcing the relay to take a circuitous journey across the Baltic Sea to Sweden and then to Finland. Instead of living in the Olympic Village with the other athletes, the Soviet and other Iron Curtain teams were lodged in Otaniemi, Finland, near a Soviet-owned naval base. Accentuating their separateness from the other athletes, these teams lived behind barbed-wire fences and beneath huge portraits of the Soviet premier, Joseph Stalin.

Although the Soviets immediately dominated many sports, they were not quite ready to challenge the Americans in track and field.

Three months earlier Lindy Remigino had wanted to quit the Manhattan College team, but Coach George Eastment convinced him to continue. At the Olympic trials he qualified in the 100 only because Andy Stanfield had chosen to concentrate on the 200 and Jim Golliday of Northwestern had withdrawn with muscle pulls. But bursting down the outside lane in the Olympic final, Remigino nipped Herb McKenley of Jamaica by inches in a photo finish.

"Do you think," he was asked, "you could've beaten Stanfield and Golliday?"

"Are you kidding?" he said. "If they were in the race, I wouldn't be here."

The most theatrical American-Russian duel developed in the 3,000-meter steeplechase, a race of slightly less than two miles over a grass course with hurdles, one of which was the water jump. Below the far side of the brush-covered hurdle, the water was knee-high; then it graded upward for at least 10 feet. Most steeplechasers cleared the hurdle, landed in the deep water, then thrashed their way out. But at the Olympic training track one day Horace Ashenfelter, a twenty-nine-year-old Federal Bureau of Investigation agent representing the New York Athletic Club, noticed that Olavi Rinteenpää of Finland balanced himself momentarily atop the hurdle on his right foot, then pushed off beyond the deep water.

"You land in the shallow water," the Finn explained. "You save time. You save energy."

The tip wasn't expected to make much difference. Vladimir Kazantsev, a Soviet from Kiev in the Ukraine, was the overwhelming favorite. Ashenfelter, a wiry five-ten and 140 pounds, had always been an undistinguished distance runner, but if he did well, maybe he could salvage a silver medal. On the final lap Kazantsev surged into the lead, with Ashenfelter close behind. At the water jump the Russian cleared the barrier, splashed into the deep water, and floundered. Ashenfelter perched atop the hurdle momentarily, pushed off, landed in the shallow area, and quickly scrambled out.

Sprinting to the finish line, Ashenfelter won easily in a world record 8:54.4. Moments later Kazantsev embraced the American in congratulations before a Soviet official led the silver medalist away. Maybe the Soviet leaders didn't adhere to the Olympic spirit, but Kazantsev had.

Arms swinging, mouth gasping for breath, Emil Zátopek lurches to the lead in the 5,000 at Helsinki.

More than anybody else, a twenty-nine-year-old Czechoslo-vakian military officer hypnotized the Helsinki spectators. Emil Zátopek had won the 10,000-meter run in London, but after finishing second in the 5,000, he trained even harder. Wearing heavy army boots, he jogged, then sprinted, then jogged at least 10 miles every day, sometimes 20 or 25 miles. But after winning the 10,000 in Helsinki, he was disappointed.

"I was not fast," he said. "I was bad, very bad. I will try to do better in the 5,000."

Not since Hannes Kolehmainen of Finland in 1912 had anyone taken the gold medals in both the 5,000 and 10,000 in the same Olympics, but now, forty years later, Kolehmainen was watching Zátopek hurrying along unlike any other runner.

"Bobbing, weaving, staggering, gyrating, clutching his torso, flinging a supplicating glance toward the heavens," sports columnist Red Smith wrote, "he ran like a man with a noose around his neck."

The noose was really around the necks of his rivals. Zátopek won the 5,000, watched his wife, Dana, win the women's javelin, then announced that he would enter the Olympic marathon. But he had never run a marathon.

"Do you really think that you can win your first marathon?" he was asked.

"If I didn't think I could win," he said, "I would not have entered."

After fifteen miles Zátopek, Gustav Jansson of Sweden, and Jim Peters of Great Britain were bunched far in front of the other runners. Zátopek slowed down, allowing Peters to catch him.

"Excuse me," said Zátopek, who spoke five languages. "I haven't run a marathon before, but don't you think we ought to go a bit faster?"

Peters soon developed cramps and dropped out. Zátopek won by more than two minutes, completing a gold-medal triple that has never been duplicated. But he didn't seem impressed by his feat.

"The marathon," he declared, "is a very boring race."

As the Olympics continued, Zátopek was upstaged by the U.S.-Soviet rivalry. The Russians took an early lead with victories in women's track and field, gymnastics, and wrestling. But in the final days American swimmers and divers, boxers (notably Floyd Paterson, later the world heavyweight champion), and weight lifters, responding to the challenge of the political cold war rivalry with the Russians, pushed the United States ahead in the final team standings, 614–553½.

Toni Sailer's Triple

In the Winter Games at Oslo six months earlier nineteen-year-old Andrea Mead Lawrence, from the Vermont mountains, had swept the women's slalom and giant slalom. Not many noticed that a skier named Christian Pravda won two medals, but in Kitzbühel, Austria, teenager Toni Sailer did.

Inspired by his hometown idol's accomplishment, Sailer "put myself on skis and just let go" in the 1956 Winter Games at Cortina d'Ampezzo in the Italian Alps. Only twenty years old, the son of the village glazier had developed into what the Austrian team coach, Fred Rossner, described as "the perfect skier—the perfect athlete in perfect condition with perfect technique." Hollywood handsome at six feet and 174 pounds, he was the first Alpine skier to complete a gold-medal triple: the downhill, slalom, and giant slalom.

"I like downhill racing the best," he said. "In the slalom, you have to brake all the time. I like to run free into the wind."

Hayes Alan Jenkins and Tenley Albright whirled to the figure skating gold medals for the United States, while the Soviets, in their first Winter Olympics, took the team title with 120 points. One of their six gold medals occurred in ice hockey, a game never played seriously in Russia until a decade earlier.

Toni Sailer winning his second of three golds at Cortina d'Ampezzo

Melbourne's Water Polo War

At the 1956 Summer Games in Melbourne, Australia (held in late November, which is summer in the Southern Hemisphere), the Soviets' obsession with the team title would resume.

"Classification by points on a national basis," the IOC decreed, "is not recognized."

Not recognized by the IOC perhaps, but recognized by the dominant nations.

Bobby Morrow, a sprinter from Abilene Christian College, doubled in the 100 and 200 and added a third gold medal as a member of the 4 x 100 relay. The U.S. basketball team, with Bill Russell and K. C. Jones (both of whom later starred in the National Basketball Association for the Boston Celtics and also coached that team), breezed to the gold medal, but overall the Soviets outscored the Americans, 722–593 in points, 37–32 in gold medals.

Another 1956 moment has endured in Olympic lore. Not long before the opening ceremony at the Melbourne Cricket Grounds, Soviet tanks rumbled into Budapest, crushing the Hungarian Revolution. But the Hungarian athletes were already on their way to Australia.

In the water polo tournament the Soviets and the defending champion Hungarians were on a collision course. In the semifinals Hungary was ahead, 4–0, when blood could be seen in the water. Valentin Prokopov had butted Ervin Zádor of Hungary, opening a deep cut near the right eye. During a time-out the Hungarians gathered at one end of the pool, but the Soviets decided to depart, forfeiting the match. Hungary went on to win the gold.

For most athletes, the Olympics created a bond. At the closing ceremony in Melbourne, instead of marching by national teams, many athletes intermingled. And at the 1960 Winter Olympics in snowy Squaw Valley, California, the Soviets' best hockey player helped the United States win a surprising gold.

Quietly the untouted U.S. team, with goaltender Jack McCartan making acrobatic saves, had upset the Soviets, 3–2, on two goals by Billy Christian of Warroad, Minnesota, but after two periods of the final Czechoslovakia was leading, 4–3. During the intermission the Soviet captain, defenseman Nikolai Sologubov, knocked on the door of the Americans' dressing room. Jack Riley, the American coach, waved him in. Sologubov didn't speak English, but his sign language was obvious.

"He wants us to use oxygen," one of the Americans said.

With renewed stamina the Americans streaked to six goals in the final period for a 9–4 victory and the gold. Cynics suggested that Sologubov had not wanted the Americans to win so much as he wanted the rival Czechs to lose. Whatever his reason, the oxygen helped.

Rome's Decathlon Duel

For all his chatter at the 1960 Summer Games in Rome, Cassius Marcellus Clay, an eighteen-year-old boxer from Louisville, Kentucky, didn't need oxygen. Known later as Muhammad Ali, he was to reign as the only three-time world heavyweight champion, earn more than sixty million dollars, and emerge as arguably the world's most recognizable personality. After winning the light heavyweight gold in Rome, he wore his medal for the next forty-eight hours.

"First time I ever slept on my back," he said. "Had to, or that medal would've cut my chest."

But the streets of Rome did not cut the toughened soles of Abebe Bikila's feet. The little Ethiopian, a member of Haile Selassie's palace guard, ran barefoot to the marathon gold.

The decathlon dwindled down to a dramatic duel between two UCLA products. C. K. Yang, twenty-seven, from what is now known as Taiwan, had won all six of the previous running and jumping events, while his friend Rafer Johnson, a twenty-six-year-old Californian, had won all three weight throwing events for a 67-point lead. If Yang could finish ten seconds ahead of Johnson in the 1,500, he would win. Running in the same heat, Yang moved in front, but Johnson dogged him.

"I could see him behind me at the turns," Yang said later. "I knew he would never let go of me unless he collapsed."

Johnson didn't collapse. Yang completed the 1,500 in 4:48.5, but when Johnson finished in 4:49.7, only 1.2 seconds later, he had earned enough points to win: 8,392–8,334. Soon after Vassily Kuznyetsov finished third, the Soviet athlete asked Johnson to pose for a photo with him.

"Sure," said Johnson, "you and me and Yang."

Kuznyetsov blinked. Taiwan, also known as Nationalist China, was politically opposed to Communist China, a Soviet ally. But the memory of the moment would be more important to Kuznyetsov than politics.

Wearing his Olympic warm-up jacket, Cassius Clay, later known as Muhammad Ali, punches the heavy bag in 1960.

"Okay," the Russian said, smiling at Yang, "but remember, I don't know you."

Although the cold war was still icy, the track-and-field competitors from the United States and the Soviet Union had come to know one another by the time the 5,902 athletes from eighty-four nations gathered for the 1960 Summer Games. Meets at Philadelphia in 1958 and Moscow in 1959 had brought them closer together.

When the Soviets had dominated the Melbourne Olympics, accumulating 807½ points to America's 564½ and forty-three gold

Rafer Johnson (center), with his decathlon gold medal, joins C. K. Yang (left) and Vassily Kuznyetsov at Rome.

medals to thirty-four, even the chairman of the Soviet Olympic Committee was gracious. "Politics is one thing, sports is another," Constantin Andrianov said. "We are sportsmen."

Skilled sportsmen. The Soviets had forced the United States to share the glory of the Olympics.

Terrorists and Black Gloves

IN THE DARKNESS BEFORE DAWN ON TUESDAY, SEPTEMBER 5, 1972, in Munich, West Germany, eight men wearing warm-up suits and carrying equipment bags scaled the eight-foot fence surrounding the Olympic Village, where the Summer Games athletes and coaches were sleeping. With a smile security guards ignored what they thought were curfew breakers, but the eight were members of the Black September terrorist group, linked to the Palestine Liberation Organization.

Hiding in an alley, the terrorists slipped Kalashnikov submachine guns out of their bags. Minutes later, after a knock on the door of an upstairs suite, one asked in German, "Is this the Israeli team?"

Awakened, an Israeli coach got up and opened the door. Seeing a submachine gun, he tried to close the door while yelling to alert

Wearing a makeshift mask, a Black September terrorist peers from the balcony outside the Israeli quarters in Munich's Olympic Village.

others in the suite. In a burst of bullets the coach was shot dead. Some athletes escaped, but when a weight lifter tried to hold off the intruders with a knife, he was shot. Soon nine Israelis were roped to the beds as hostages.

What became known as the Munich Massacre, the bloodiest stain on Olympic history, had begun.

Police in armored cars surrounded the Olympic Village as the terrorists demanded that in exchange for the nine hostages, more than two hundred Arab guerrillas be released from Israeli prisons. They also demanded a jetliner to take them and the hostages to an undisclosed destination. But in Israel the cabinet decided not to negotiate. West Germany's Foreign Ministry contacted various Arab nations, but none offered to mediate.

Meanwhile, the specter of terrorists in ski masks on an Olympic Village balcony was seen on television all over the world. Suddenly the Olympics were much more than a sports carnival.

By sunset German officials had arranged for two helicopters to take the terrorists and the hostages to a nearby air base, where a Boeing 727 jet was waiting. When some of the terrorists stepped out of one of the helicopters to check the jet, sharpshooters opened fire. Three terrorists were hit. Another took cover; then he shot out the air control tower lights. Still another tossed a hand grenade that exploded in one of the helicopters holding several bound hostages.

When the hour-long firefight ended, five Arab terrorists were dead, along with one German policeman and the nine Israeli hostages in addition to the two Israelis killed in the original attack.

"The greater and more important the Olympic Games become," the outgoing IOC president, Avery Brundage, said, "the more they are open to commercial, political, and now criminal pressure."

The deaths of eleven members of the Israeli team (six wrestlers and weight lifters as well as five coaches) shrouded the Olympics in sadness. Many observers believed that Brundage should have canceled the remaining four days of competition, but after a memorial service (ignored by the Arab and Soviet athletes) in the stadium on Wednesday, the Summer Games resumed the next day.

Mark Spitz's Seven Golds

Before the Olympics were bloodied, twenty-two-year-old swimmer Mark Spitz had stood on the gold-medal platform a record seven times.

Spitz either set an individual world record or anchored a relay record in his seven events: 200 butterfly, 400 freestyle relay, 200 freestyle, 100 butterfly, 800 freestyle relay, 100 freestyle, and 400 medley relay. After earning his seventh gold medal, Spitz was escorted to a news conference to discuss his Olympic triumphs on what turned out to be the same morning that the Arab terrorists were holding the Israelis hostage. Suddenly the questions were not what he had expected.

"The press wanted my words," he said later, "because, first, I was Jewish, and second, they thought I was some kind of spokesman for athletes."

Because of the terrorist attack, the IOC and the State Department agreed that it was too dangerous for such an internationally celebrated Jewish swimmer to remain in Munich. He soon returned home. But before and after the Israeli deaths these Summer Games had problems.

The afternoon of the 100-meter quarterfinals Eddie Hart and Rey Robinson were in the Olympic Village with Stan Wright, their sprint coach. Each shared the world record with a time of 9.9, but when they glanced at a nearby television set, they noticed sprinters lining up for a heat.

"Must be a rerun of the morning heats," Robinson mentioned.

"No, this is live," a bystander explained.

"Oh, no," Hart said. "That's the heat I'm supposed to be in."

Wright, who had checked an outdated schedule, had mistakenly told the two sprinters that they would be running at seven o'clock that evening when their heat had been moved up to four-thirty in the

The shot heard 'round the basketball world: Aleksandr Belov's lay-up for the Soviet Union concluded the controversial 51–50 defeat of the U.S. team at Munich.

afternoon. Wright accepted the blame, but both sprinters were disqualified for their absences. Hart later anchored the 4 x 100 relay's gold medal.

Rick DeMont, a sixteen-year-old high school senior from San Rafael, California, won the 400-meter freestyle, but he was disqualified when a banned drug, ephedrine, was discovered in his urine sample. Afflicted with asthma, he had been prescribed medication that included ephedrine. He had specified the drug on his Olympic application.

But the USOC bungled De-Mont's appeal. He not only had to return his gold medal but also was barred from competing in the 1,500 freestyle.

As if these two situations weren't embarrassing enough, the American basketball team endured a controversial defeat. Never had the United States lost an Olympic basketball game. And when Doug Collins hit two free throws for a 50–49 lead over the Soviet Union with three seconds remaining, the streak seemed safe. When the Soviets' inbounds pass was deflected, the Americans celebrated until the Bulgarian and Brazilian referees cleared the court, ruling that one second remained. After another inbounds pass was short, the Americans again assumed they had won.

Then the British secretary-general of the International Amateur Basketball Federation, Dr. R. William Jones, ordered the clocks reset at three seconds.

Awaiting the third length-of-the-court inbounds pass, Kevin Joyce and James Forbes surrounded Aleksandr Belov, the six-eight Russian center, who was parked in the three-second lane. Under international rules the three-second count on a player in the lane begins as soon as the ball is handed to the inbounds passer. The two referees ignored Belov's violation. They also ignored Belov's knocking Forbes to the floor as he grabbed Ivan Edeshko's inbounds pass and banked in a lay-up at the buzzer for a 51–50 Soviet victory, ending the United States's sixty-three-game streak.

Coach Hank Iba filed a protest that was disallowed, but the players decided on another form of protest. They refused their silver medals.

"We know we won it," said Bobby Jones, later a star forward with the Philadelphia 76ers, "and everybody in the U.S. knows we won it."

For the first time since 1908 the marathon was won by an American, Frank Shorter, who coincidentally had been born in Munich when his father was an army doctor stationed there. Overall the United States earned ninety-four medals (thirty-three gold), second to the Soviet Union's ninety-nine medals (fifty gold).

"This shows the entire world," the Soviet newspaper *Pravda* bragged, "the triumph of the personality liberated by socialism."

Sapporo's Ski Scandal

But more and more Olympic athletes were being liberated by capitalism. Before the 1972 Winter Games in Sapporo, Japan, the IOC, reacting to whispers that several celebrated skiers were receiving at least fifty thousand dollars a year in "expenses" from meet pro-

**As graceful as a swan,
Peggy Fleming glides to
the gold at Grenoble.**

moters, banned Karl Schranz of Austria, the favorite in the three men's Alpine events.

"Schranz talked too much," said Marc Hodler, the International Ski Federation president.

Schranz had flouted the Olympic amateur code by accepting cash payments, as track-and-field athletes had done for decades. In the years that followed, the IOC was to ignore the hundreds of thousands of dollars paid to world-class skiers and track-and-field athletes, knowing that if it were to ban them, those Olympic sports would be barren.

Japan also was the site of the 1964 Summer Games when Bob Hayes, later an All-NFL wide receiver with the Dallas Cowboys, won the 100 and anchored the 4 x 100 relay. Billy Mills, a virtually unknown U.S. Marine lieutenant who was part Sioux Native American, thundered down the stretch in the 10,000 to nip the world-record holder, Ron Clarke of Australia.

"Were you worried about Mills?" the Aussie was asked later.

"Worried about him?" Clarke replied. "I never heard of him."

In the 1964 Winter Games at Innsbruck, Austria, speed skater Lydia Skoblikova of the Soviet Union won four gold medals, but Terry McDermott, a Bay City, Michigan, barber, stunned the Russian favorite, Yevgeni Grishin, in the men's 500. In 1968 at Grenoble, France, Peggy Fleming regained the women's figure skating gold medal for the United States, and Jean-Claude Killy emerged as the idol of the host nation with a sweep of the three men's Alpine events: the downhill, slalom, and giant slalom.

Mexico City's Controversy

In the months preceding the 1968 Summer Games in Mexico City, the Olympic stage was smeared by politics. South Africa, barred by the IOC in 1964 for its apartheid policy, was readmitted, then rebarred. Student riots in Mexico City resulted in forty-nine deaths. In the United States, meanwhile, black activists in the civil rights movement proposed an Olympic boycott by black American athletes. Lew Alcindor, the UCLA basketball center later known as Kareem Abdul-Jabbar, joined the boycott.

Two other American athletes, Tommie Smith and John Carlos, silently created a much louder protest at Mexico City.

Minutes after the 200-meter final, their heads bowed during the playing of "The Star-Spangled Banner," gold medalist Smith and bronze medalist Carlos each lifted a black-gloved fist symbolizing black unity and black power. Smith wore a black scarf, and Carlos black beads, to signify black lynchings. Both stood in black stockinged feet, representing black poverty. Most of the eighty-thousand people in the Olympic Stadium didn't understand the significance of the protest. Others booed.

"It was not a gesture of hate," Smith has explained. "It was a gesture of frustration."

Spurred by Brundage and the IOC, the USOC branded the gesture "discourteous...untypical exhibitionism...immature behavior." Smith and Carlos were suspended from the U.S. team and evicted from the Olympic Village. But to many American blacks in that time of struggles over basic civil rights and over the Vietnam War, what Smith and Carlos did was courageous, timely, and responsible.

"The juice, the fire of '68, that scared a lot of people," Carlos said years later. "It scared government and business. It still scares them."

Smith and Carlos had made a statement remembered negatively by some, glowingly by others. But in Mexico City black American athletes had other moments. Lee Evans, Larry James, and Ron Freeman, who finished one, two, three in the 400, wore black berets to the medal platform but removed them during the national anthem. Heavyweight boxer George Foreman celebrated his gold medal by waving a small American flag in the ring. Bob Beamon, a long-legged long jumper, soared 29 feet, 2½ inches through Mexico City's rarefied air, breaking the world record by nearly two feet. In the landing pit he covered his face with his hands.

With black gloves to the sky, Tommie Smith (center) and John Carlos protest at Mexico City.

"I was thanking that Man up there," he said later, "for letting me hit the ground where He did."

Of all the Olympians in Mexico City, discus thrower Al Oerter, an aircraft computer analyst representing the New York Athletic Club, was the one who achieved a track-and-field first: a fourth consecutive gold medal. And each time he had not been the favorite.

"I get fired up for the Olympics," he explained. "Something happens to me. The people, the pressure, everything about the Olympics is special to me."

Through worldwide television the Olympics also were special to more and more people, more and more athletes (a record 7,886 from 112 nations in twenty-seven sports at Mexico City), more and more commercial sponsors, more and more politicians. As two black-gloved fists at Mexico City and eleven dead members of the Israeli team at Munich proved, the Olympics had become a stage for protest and power.

The Miracle in Lake Placid

FOR NEARLY SIX MONTHS THE U.S. OLYMPIC HOCKEY players had listened to Herb Brooks's pep talks.

"We went to the well again," their coach had often said. "The water was colder; the water was deeper."

Never had the water been colder or deeper than now. In a few minutes the U.S. team was to oppose the Soviet Union, arguably the world's best hockey team, in the 1980 Winter Games at Lake Placid, New York. The year before, the Soviets had conquered the National Hockey League all-stars in a best two-of-three Challenge Cup series, including a 6–0 strafing in the decisive third game. In the U.S. team's last Olympic tune-up, these collegians and castoffs from Massachusetts and Minnesota had been routed by the Soviets, 10–3. Not that Herb Brooks was about to surrender.

"You were born to be a hockey player," the coach told his team in the locker room. "This is your moment and it's going to happen. You were meant to be here."

His Olympic team was there with a 4–0–1 record, salvaging an opening 2–2 tie with Sweden before sweeping to four victories: 7–3 over Czechoslovakia, 5–1 over Norway, 7–2 over Romania, and 4–3 over West Germany. But with a 5–0 record the Russians were unbeaten, untied, and unmerciful: 16–0 over Japan, 17–4 over the Netherlands, 8–1 over Poland, 4–2 over Finland, and 6–4 over Canada.

In the Olympic Field House, fans were waving American flags and chanting, "USA! USA!" as they had throughout the tournament. But when the Russians took a quick 1–0 lead, then 2–1, the outcome appeared inevitable. Suddenly, in the final second of the first period, Mark Johnson, the son of the 1976 Olympic hockey coach, slipped the puck past goaltender Vladislav Tretiak.

When the Russians, in their red and white uniforms, skated out for the second period, Vladimir Myshkin glided to the net. Tretiak had been benched by Viktor Tikhonov, the Soviet coach. Myshkin was a good goaltender, but many hockey experts considered Tretiak the best goaltender ever, better than any of the best in the NHL. The other Russian players were shocked by Tikhonov's decision.

"We couldn't believe it," Vyacheslav Fetisov, later a defenseman with the New Jersey Devils, has said. "Tretiak was the best."

Sticks and spirits high, the U.S. hockey team celebrates its upset of the Soviet Union at Lake Placid.

When the Russians took a 3–2 lead into the third period, Tretiak's absence didn't seem to matter. But then Mark Johnson created a 3–3 tie, and with exactly ten minutes remaining, left winger Mike Eruzione, the U.S. captain from Winthrop, Massachusetts, scored for a 4–3 lead. In the closing minutes the Russians skated desperately, but Tikhonov never pulled Myshkin to insert a sixth shooter. As the final seconds flashed, Al Michaels spoke into his ABC microphone.

"Do you," he asked his worldwide television audience, "believe in miracles?"

Maybe it wasn't a miracle, but the U.S. team's 4–3 victory was arguably the most memorable upset not only in Olympic history but in sports history. If the U.S. and Soviet teams had played twenty hockey games, maybe the United States would have won one. Maybe. But this was that one. And this was the one that counted. Outside the Olympic Field House fireworks lit up the sky above the snow-muddied streets of the Adirondack mountain village. All over America people would remember where they were and what they were doing when they heard the news.

America needed something to cheer about. Inflation was spiraling. In Iran dozens of American hostages were being held in the U.S. Embassy. Soviet troops were in Afghanistan, provoking a threat by President Jimmy Carter to boycott the Summer Games in Moscow.

But to win the hockey gold medal, the U.S. team had to defeat Finland in Sunday's final game. If the United States lost, it would finish fourth. For the seventh time in their seven games, the Americans fell behind, until three goals in the third period produced a 4–2 victory. When the buzzer sounded, they hugged, tossed their sticks and gloves to the people who were chanting "USA! USA!" and danced with those who had skidded onto the ice with American flags, large and small, as goaltender Jim Craig wrapped himself in one of the flags.

At a White House reception for the Winter Olympic team the next day, Eric Heiden, the speed skater who had won a record five gold medals, objected to a possible boycott of the Summer Games.

In his gold speed-skating suit, Eric Heiden strides to the 1,000 gold at Lake Placid.

"I hope we don't boycott," Heiden said after President Carter had reiterated his stand in his remarks. "The winter athletes in general just don't feel that a boycott is the right thing."

Heiden had done what no other speed skater had ever done. He had won all five of the men's events at 500, 1,000, 1,500, 5,000, and 10,000 meters, the equivalent of a runner's winning the 100, the

400, the 800, the 1,500, and the 5,000. But in all the excitement over the hockey team he had been upstaged. Not that he minded.

"It saved me a lot of hassles," he said later. "I don't have to worry about people knowing who I am."

The Moscow Boycott

In the years that followed, Heiden all but disappeared. He soon stopped skating competitively and turned to cycling, winning the United States pro championship. Now an orthopedist specializing in sports medicine and an occasional speed skating television analyst, Heiden accepted only three of dozens of commercial offers after Lake Placid—for sportswear, toothpaste, and bicycles. At the 1980 Olympic cycling trials he qualified as an alternate, but he never went to Moscow; neither did any other American athletes. More than thirty other nations joined the U.S. boycott. They included West Germany, Japan, Canada, the People's Republic of China, and the Republic of China.

Some U.S. athletes—notably gymnast Kurt Thomas, hurdler Renaldo Nehemiah, boxer Johnny Bumphus, and basketball players Isiah Thomas, Buck Williams, Rolando Blackman, and Carol Blazejowski—lost their Olympic opportunities.

"You train all your life," Thomas said years later, "but there's no way you can prepare for something like that. I didn't bad-mouth the President. I didn't sound bad, but I felt bad. But I'm not bitter. I've never been that way. At the time I wasn't happy about it, but you have to go on."

Without the United States there, the Soviets won a record eighty gold medals, three by swimmer Vladimir Salnikov. Three British athletes prevailed: Daley Thompson in the decathlon, Sebastian Coe in the 1,500, and Steve Ovett in the 800. Teófilo Stevenson of Cuba won his third heavyweight boxing gold medal.

With the increasing influence of politics, the U.S.-inspired boycott of Moscow was not the first Olympic boycott. Nor was it the last.

Montreal's Moneymen

At the 1976 Summer Games in Montreal the emerging African nations had objected to a New Zealand rugby team's tour of South Africa. When the IOC declined to bar New Zealand, twenty-four African and Caribbean countries departed, reducing the total competitors to 9,121 from ninety-two nations. But the new IOC president, Lord Killanin of Ireland, supported Canada's argument that only one Chinese delegation be recognized, the People's Republic of China, also known as Communist China, and that the Republic of China, also known as Taiwan, be ordered to go home. Canada, incidentally, had recently signed a multimillion-dollar wheat deal with the People's Republic.

Montreal's politics also created financial debts that still haunt its taxpayers. Olympic costs were budgeted at $310 million but escalated to $1.2 billion because of poor planning, inflation, and labor delays.

In the Olympic Village of high-rise apartment houses that later were rented by Montreal residents, athletes and visitors were screened by metal detectors following the massacre of eleven Israeli team members in Munich.

One of that Olympics' youngest competitors, fourteen-year-old Nadia Comaneci of Romania, dazzled the world. Never before had a gymnast received a perfect 10 until this four-foot-eleven-inch eighty-six-pound athlete earned seven 10s in winning three gold medals in the all-around, balance beam, and uneven bars. Five American boxers also triumphed: light heavyweight Leon Spinks, middleweight Michael Spinks, light welterweight Sugar Ray Leonard, lightweight Howard Davis, and flyweight Leo Randolph.

Bruce Jenner, whose wife, Chrystie, worked as an airline flight attendant to support his training, won the decathlon, and another Californian, swimmer John Naber, earned four gold medals. So did swimmer Kornelia Ender, one of many East Germans suspected of using steroids.

"I still ask myself," Ender said after the fall of the German

With a
left-handed
lunge,
Bruce Jenner
tosses the
shot at
Montreal.

Democratic Republic in 1991, "whether it could be possible they gave me things, because I remember being given injections during training and competition. But this was explained to me as being substances to help me regenerate and recuperate. Medical men are the real guilty people. They know what they have done. When they gave us things to help us 'regenerate,' we were never asked if we wanted it. It was just given."

Although the Soviets again won the most medals—125, including 47 golds—East Germany finished second in the medal standings with 90, including 40 golds. America had 34 golds.

Montreal's debt contrasted with that of Innsbruck, Austria, the Winter Games site in 1976 for the second time in twelve years. Only $148 million was spent there, most of it on permanent venues. Sheila Young, a speed skater from Detroit, Michigan, sold her fiancé's bicycle for $250 to pay his airfare to Innsbruck, and it was worth it. She won three events in three days: gold in the 500, silver in the 3,000, bronze in the 1,500.

In the 1984 Winter Games at Sarajevo, Yugoslavia, figure skaters Scott Hamilton, a toy bulldog from Bowling Green, Ohio, and East Germany's Katarina Witt took the golds. Debbie Armstrong provided the United States with a women's gold in the giant slalom after Billy Johnson, a cocky Californian, stunned the European downhill racers.

Scott Hamilton, the gold medalist at Sarajevo

"I'm going to smoke 'em," Johnson predicted. He did just that, the first American to win the Olympic downhill.

And not long after Phil Mahre and his twin brother, Steve, finished one, two in the slalom, the gold medalist learned that his wife had given birth to a boy in Phoenix, Arizona. Asked what he would be doing a year later, Phil laughed.

"Probably baby-sitting," he said.

Carl Lewis's Four Golds

Five months later the 1984 Summer Games in Los Angeles had inspired another boycott, this time by the Soviet Union (in reprisal for the U.S. boycott of Moscow) and other Communist-bloc nations. In their absence U.S. athletes roared to eighty-three gold medals. Carl Lewis duplicated Jesse Owens's feat, winning the same four events. He took the 100 in 9.9. The next day he coasted through two qualifying heats in the 200, then leaped 28 feet, ½ inch on his first long jump. He fouled on his second jump. When nobody else approached his distance, he didn't take his third jump. Unwilling to risk injury by going for Bob Beamon's world record of 29 feet, 2½ inches, he departed to boos from many of the 85,870 spectators in the Los Angeles Coliseum.

"It got cold very quickly," he explained later. "I was a little sore after the second jump. I didn't want to risk it."

Lewis added the 200 gold medal in 19.8, then anchored the 4 x 100 relay to the gold medal in a world-record 37.83 seconds. Valerie Brisco-Hooks doubled in the women's 200 and 400. Evelyn Ashford darted to the gold in the 100. America's best woman distance runner, Mary Decker, fell in the 3,000 in a tangle with Zola Budd of South Africa. Decker angrily blamed the barefoot Budd but later changed her mind.

"It will be with me for a long time," Decker said, "but it was an accident."

Michael Jordan, Patrick Ewing, and Chris Mullin were the best

As if wearing wings, Mary Lou Retton soars to the all-around gold at Los Angeles.

players on Coach Bobby Knight's gold-medal basketball team. Rowdy Gaines, denied a chance to swim at Moscow by the boycott, splashed to three gold medals, including the 100 freestyle; Tracy Caulkins, Mary T. Meagher, and Nancy Hogshead each also won three golds.

"I'd swim another eight years and go through another boycott for this feeling," Gaines said. "This makes it all worthwhile."

Joan Benoit won the first Olympic women's marathon, and a sixteen-year-old West Virginian, Mary Lou Retton, charmed America, if not the world. Needing a 10 on either of her vaults to win the all-around gold medal from Ecaterina Szabo of Romania, she walked over to her coach, Bela Karolyi.

"I'm going to stick it," she said.

After sprinting to the launching board, up and around and down she came, landing without a wobble. Quickly she raised both arms and smiled. Moments later the electronic scoreboard flashed "10."

Mary Lou Retton had stuck it for her gold medal in the first Olympics to sell sponsorships to multimillion-dollar corporations. Under the direction of Peter Ueberroth, later the baseball commissioner, these 1984 Summer Games were also the first Olympics to earn a profit—a dazzling $215 million.

More than ever before, the Olympics were now big business.

Michael Jordan (center) enjoys the gold-medal ceremony at Barcelona with Scottie Pippen (left) and Clyde Drexler.

The Dream Team

ON AN OLD NARROW STREET IN OLD DOWNTOWN Barcelona, hundreds of people had been gathering for hours to see basketball's Dream Team. But not in a game. They were there for the arrival of the U.S. Olympic players at the Hotel Ambassador, where their rooms cost nine hundred dollars a night. Now, beyond the flashing lights of police motorcycles, the buses were sighted.

"Here they come," somebody yelled.

One by one three chartered buses stopped in front of the hotel entrance guarded by Spanish *policia*. Coach Chuck Daly, the first off, was applauded, but when Michael Jordan and Earvin ("Magic") Johnson appeared, cheers thundered through the old narrow street.

"Michael! Michael!" the people were yelling. "Magic! Magic!"

These basketball Beatles symbolized the new Olympic era of professional athletes competing with the approval of their sports' international federations. When the International Basketball Federation ruled that pros would be eligible for the 1992 Summer Games and other international tournaments, a group known as USA Basketball, stung by the 1988 bronze-medal disappointment of the U.S. team, assembled eleven of the National Basketball Association's best players and another about to be an NBA rookie: Michael Jordan, Magic Johnson, Larry Bird, Patrick Ewing, David Robinson, Charles Barkley, Karl Malone, Chris Mullin, Scottie Pippen, Clyde Drexler, John Stockton, and Christian Laettner.

Magic Johnson had stopped playing for the Los Angeles Lakers nearly a year earlier after learning he had contracted the virus that causes AIDS, but as a fans' selection for the NBA All-Star Game he had been its most valuable player. Jordan, of course, was considered the world's best player, having led the Chicago Bulls to two consecutive NBA titles (the following year the Bulls won their third straight title).

The outcome of the Olympic tournament was never in doubt. The Dream Team won as easily as Jordan dunked a basketball. It routed Croatia in the gold-medal game, 117-85, after streaking through Angola, Croatia, Germany, Brazil, Spain, Puerto Rico, and Lithuania.

Chuck Daly juggled all those NBA egos masterfully, but the coach credited the Dream Team's success to "peer pressure," the responsibility each all-star put on the others to perform as well as possible no matter what the quality of opposition. Jordan credited Magic Johnson with being "able to blend the egos," but Barkley summed it up best.

"This has been one of the greatest experiences for everybody," the Phoenix Suns' forward said. "Everybody here was cheering for everybody else."

Not quite everybody. Dr. LeRoy Walker, the incoming USOC president, complained about the Dream Team's being lodged in a downtown hotel instead of participating in the Olympic Village experience.

"They should follow the same rules as everybody else," Walker said. "If they don't want to, and aren't here next time, I wouldn't care."

But the IOC president, Juan Antonio Samaranch, thanked David Stern, the NBA commissioner, for the boost to the Olympics' worldwide popularity that the Dream Team provided. Samaranch had favored opening the Olympics to professional athletes rather than tolerating the hypocrisy that many so-called amateurs, especially world-class track-and-field athletes and skiers, were millionaires with appearance fees and commercial contracts.

One of those millionaires, Carl Lewis, raised his career total of gold medals to eight, winning the long jump and anchoring the 4 x 100 relay. Gail Devers, recovered from a thyroid ailment known as Graves' disease, took the women's 100.

Cuban boxers, returning to the Olympics for the first time since 1980 at Moscow, won seven golds. Oscar de la Hoya, a light fly-weight, was the only American boxer to survive new computer-scoring problems that seemed to confuse some judges.

In many respects the Summer Games had never been bigger or better, as a record 10,563 athletes from 171 nations competed in 257 events in forty-three sports, watched by an estimated 3.5 billion television viewers. But the real beauty of Barcelona was that for the first time since 1972, the Summer Games were truly a world event.

Much of the politics that had created boycotts in 1976, 1980, 1984, and 1988 was no longer a factor. In 1989 the Berlin Wall had been torn down, allowing the athletes from West Germany and East Germany to merge into one team. In 1991 the Soviet Union had collapsed, allowing twelve former Soviet republics to form a one-time-only Unified Team that accumulated a total of 112 medals in Barcelona; the United States earned 108. South Africa, its apartheid politics outlawed, returned after a thirty-two-year ban.

Ben Johnson's Steroids

Equally important, the Olympics rebounded from the embarrassment of the 1988 Summer Games in Seoul, South Korea, when Ben Johnson set a world record of 9.79 in the 100-meter dash.

"This world record will last fifty years, maybe one hundred," said the Canadian sprinter who grew up in Jamaica. "More important than the world record was to beat Carl Lewis and win the gold."

The record didn't last much more than fifty hours. Stanozolol, a banned performance-enhancing steroid, was found in Johnson's postrace urine sample. He was stripped of his gold medal (which was awarded to Lewis) and the world record; he also was suspended by the International Amateur Athletic Federation for two years. Johnson left Seoul in disgrace, but the scandal cheered some athletes.

"I want a clean sport," Mary Decker Slaney said. "The fact that a thing this big can't be swept under the rug is a sign of hope."

Arms pumping, Ben Johnson breaks away in the 100 at Seoul, before his disqualification for use of illegal steroids.

Steroids haunted Seoul that year. Of the seventeen hundred athletes tested, ten were disqualified. Two Bulgarian weight lifters were stripped of their gold medals, along with a Hungarian silver-medal weight lifter and a British bronze-medal judoist. Florence Griffith Joyner, who earned three gold medals in the 100, 200, and 4 x 100 relay, and Jackie Joyner-Kersee, who won the long jump and the heptathlon, had to defend themselves against whispers of steroids.

"I'm not on steroids," Joyner-Kersee said. "It's sad for me. I worked hard for this."

Kristin Otto, an East German swimmer, won six golds: the 50 freestyle, the 100 freestyle, the 100 backstroke, the 100 butterfly, and two relays. When several East German coaches confessed in 1991 to having slipped steroids into the meals of their swimmers, Otto defended her integrity.

"It is important," she said, "to research what really happened, to ask officials what they did. I passed every drug test, but I can't be sure what was put into my drinks and food."

Florence Griffith Joyner celebrates her 200 gold in her husband's arms at Seoul.

Alberto Tomba swoops through the giant-slalom gates at Calgary.

Boxing was embarrassed too. After a South Korean lost an early-round bout, Korean officials assaulted the New Zealand referee. Heavyweight Ray Mercer and light heavyweight Andrew Maynard earned gold medals for the United States, as did super heavyweight Lennox Lewis for Canada, but light middleweight Roy Jones, Jr., after clearly outpointing Park Si-Hun of South Korea, was deprived of the decision. As if to apologize, officials voted Jones the tournament's outstanding boxer.

Almost quietly the U.S. women's basketball team finally won a gold medal, 77–70 over Yugoslavia in the final, and swimmer Matt Biondi had three golds draped around his neck: 50 freestyle, 100 freestyle, and 4 x 100 freestyle relay.

At the 1988 Winter Games at Calgary, Alberta, in Canada, little Bonnie Blair, a pixie from Champaign, Illinois, burst onto the Olympic stage with a gold medal in the 500-meter speed skate. Another American, Brian Boitano, and East Germany's Katarina Witt took the figure skating golds. Alberto Tomba of Italy captured the slalom and the giant slalom.

When the 1992 Winter Games opened in the Alps above Albertville, France, Tomba declared it "Alberto-ville," but he had to settle for only one gold, in the giant slalom. The newly merged German team had the most medals, twenty-six, including ten golds. The Unified Team, representing twelve former Soviet republics, had twenty-three medals, including the hockey gold.

In 1994 the Olympic schedule changed. Instead of having both the Winter and Summer Games in the same year, the IOC decided to hold them two years apart. The Summer Games would resume on the usual four-year schedule in Atlanta in 1996 and Sydney, Australia, in 2000, but the next Winter Games would be held in Lillehammer, Norway, in 1994, with Nagano, Japan, the 1998 site.

The two-year gap helped Bonnie Blair win the 500 and 1,000 again for a total of five gold medals, the most of any American woman. Dan Jansen, who fell twice in 1988 and failed to win a medal in 1992, finally won the men's 1,000, while Johann Olav Koss thrilled his Norwegian followers with three gold medals in the 1,500, 5,000, and 10,000. Tommy Moe, who grew up in Whitefish, Montana, took the men's downhill, and Diann Roffe-Steinrotter won the women's super giant slalom. Cathy Turner added another short-track speed skating gold.

Nancy Kerrigan's Bruised Knee

But more than five weeks before Lillehammer's opening ceremony, the value of an Olympic victory was smeared by one of the most

Nancy Kerrigan skates to her silver at Lillehammer.

heinous crimes in sports history: deliberate injury to a rival competitor by those close to one competitor hoping for future financial gain.

After a practice session at the U.S. Figure Skating Championships in Detroit on January 6, a gold-medal favorite, Nancy Kerrigan, was walking to her dressing room in Cobo Arena when an assailant whacked her above the right knee with a black baton. Kerrigan collapsed to the floor as the assailant hurried out a back door to a waiting car.

"Why? Why? Why?" Kerrigan moaned.

Her knee bruised and battered, unsure if she would recover in time to compete in the Olympics at a level worthy of a medal, Kerrigan withdrew from the U.S. championships. Tonya Harding meanwhile finished first in the U.S. championships, clinching an Olympic berth. But police soon were investigating reports that Harding, as well as her ex-husband, Jeff Gillooly, had been involved in the plot to injure the Stoneham, Massachusetts, skater. Harding professed her innocence. Then, on January 13, police in Portland, Oregon, Harding's hometown, charged two men with conspiracy to commit a felony: Shawn Eckhardt, who had been Harding's 350-pound bodyguard, and Derrick Smith, who drove the getaway car. The next day Shane Shant, who eventually admitted to having clubbed Kerrigan, was arrested.

Two weeks later Gillooly pleaded guilty to racketeering; he received a two-year jail term and a hundred-thousand-dollar fine while telling police that Harding had helped to plan the attack.

Kerrigan soon recovered and was granted a special exemption to join the U.S. Olympic team. Harding acknowledged having learned shortly after the assault on Kerrigan that several people she knew had been involved in it; she also acknowledged that she had failed to report that information to the police. But when the USOC declined to discipline Harding immediately, she arrived in Lillehammer as Kerrigan's teammate.

Harding stumbled through the technical program, finishing tenth, while Kerrigan dazzled the judges, earning first place. In the long program Harding missed her opening jump, then informed the judges that the lace on her right skate had broken. Granted time to find another lace, she lifted herself to eighth place. Kerrigan skated better than she ever had in her life, but Oksana Baiul, a sixteen-year-old Ukrainian, won.

"It's not right, what the judges did," said Brenda Kerrigan, Nancy's mother. "But the silver medal will give Nancy back her normal life quicker."

Tonya Harding's life would never be normal. On March 16, 1994, she apologized in a Portland courtroom for "hindering prosecution," part of her plea bargain. She was placed on three years' probation, assessed $160,000 in fines and fees, and ordered to perform five hundred hours of community service. She also was ordered to resign from the U.S. Figure Skating Association and to withdraw from the world championships in Japan. Eckhardt, Shant, and Smith each were sentenced to eighteen months in jail.

"I would just like to say," Harding told the judge, "that I am really sorry I interfered."

But the Harding-Kerrigan incident showed how, in the century since their 1896 resurrection by Baron Pierre de Coubertin, the Olympics had evolved from ceremonial olive wreaths for truly amateur athletes into crass commercial competitions for many of the professional athletes. And the IOC itself had emerged as big business, extracting a total of $3.55 billion from the National Broadcasting Company for television and cable rights to the five Summer Games and Winter Games from the year 2000 to 2008.

The Olympics had lost much of their innocence, but overall they remained the world's most glorious sports spectacle.

part TWO

Wanting to Be the Best

ONE DAY WHEN CARL LEWIS WAS TEN YEARS OLD, HE won the long jump in a kids' track meet in Philadelphia, not far from his Willingboro, New Jersey, home. Presenting the medals at that 1971 meet was Jesse Owens, the winner of four gold medals in the 1936 Summer Games at Berlin.

"You're really talented," Owens told him. "You're just a little guy, but you beat all the big guys."

Two decades later Carl Lewis was six feet, two inches and a sleek 175 pounds, far from a little guy. But he was still beating all the big guys. And with a total of eight Olympic gold medals in track and field (four at Los Angeles in 1984, two each at Seoul in 1988 and at Barcelona in 1992), he had even beaten the legend of Jesse Owens himself.

If the ancient Greeks could return today to watch only one of the modern Olympians run and jump, they might well choose Carl Lewis.

"I want to be the best of all time—the best sprinter, the best long jumper," he once said. "To do that, I have to break the records."

With a blazing time of 9.86 seconds, he set the world record in the 100-meter dash at the 1991 World Championships in Tokyo.

"The best race of my life!" he shouted in celebrating the record. "The best technique, the fastest time. And I did it at thirty."

In the same meet four days later Lewis was hoping to set the world record in the long jump. For nearly a quarter of a century Bob Beamon's soaring leap of 29 feet, 2½ inches in the 1968 Summer Games at Mexico City had endured as track and field's oldest record.

**Carl Lewis soars to his
long-jump gold at Barcelona.**

Beamon never surpassed 27 feet again; his best was 26-11½. In contrast, Lewis had won sixty-five consecutive long jump competitions, with 56 leaps of 28 feet or better.

In the Tokyo final Lewis jumped 29-2¾, but it was disallowed as a record because of a following wind. Instead Mike Powell broke Beamon's record with a leap of 29-4½ when the wind wasn't blowing so hard.

Lewis was annoyed. "Mike had one great jump," he snapped. "He may never do it again." Lewis later agreed that Powell, out of Alta Loma, California, deserved the record, but the loss had rekindled his competitive flame for the 1992 Summer Games at Barcelona.

"Somebody was just telling me," he said that day in Tokyo, "that it's not time to stop jumping yet."

While on the University of Houston track team, Lewis had defied those who suggested that he couldn't excel as both a long jumper and a sprinter, that he should make a choice between those two events and then concentrate on that one event.

"For most guys," he said before the 1984 Olympics, "there's a mental block about trying to do more than one event. They're afraid of going for two and getting two seconds. But every time somebody has told me I couldn't do something, I've done it."

In 1981 Lewis was the first athlete since Jesse Owens to win a track event and a field event in national competition. In 1982 he repeated that double; in 1983 he was the first in ninety-seven years to win three outdoor titles: 100, 200, and long jump.

"Carl," his Houston coach, Tom Tellez, said, "is a long jumper who sprints."

As a sprinter Lewis practiced bursting out of the starting blocks, practiced flowing into overdrive, practiced finishing in a blaze. But as a long jumper Lewis practiced speeding down the runway, measuring his strides until the takeoff board, then rotating his legs as he sailed high and far into the sandpit.

"What I do is totally unnatural," he said. "I leave the board going almost forward. Most people go up and look beautiful in the air, but they come straight down. When I'm in the air, I rotate forward, and I fight to keep my balance or I'll fall flat on my face. That's why I use a hitch-kick to swing my balance backward."

At first Lewis used twenty-one strides to the takeoff board, but by the 1984 Olympics he was using twenty-three strides before soaring.

"Once you hit the board, it's so quick you can't remember it," he said, alluding to his takeoff speed of twenty-seven miles an hour. "Especially given how much we do in that amount of time, 1.4 seconds is too fast for the mind to think and recapture it."

When Lewis outjumped Powell in Barcelona with a leap of 28-5½, he reigned again as the Olympic champion. Powell, who earned the silver medal with 28-4¼, still held the world record, but he knew he had been upstaged again in his specialty.

"The rest of the world may see Carl Lewis a couple times a year," Powell said, "but we think about him every day."

Al Oerter's Fabulous Four

Lewis was already thinking about his 1996 opportunity to equal Al Oerter's record four consecutive gold medals in the same event. Lewis won the long jump at Los Angeles, Seoul, and Barcelona; Oerter won the discus throw at Melbourne in 1956, Rome in 1960, Tokyo in 1964, and Mexico City in 1968.

"There is something about the Olympics that gets in your blood," Oerter has said. "All those people from all those nations, all with the same purpose. The crowds, the training, the competition, the pressure. I know it may sound dumb, but I can really get charged up about the Olympics."

At Tokyo in 1964 Oerter, a muscular six-four and 275 pounds, was more charged up than ever. With a surgical collar protecting a pinched nerve in his neck and adhesive tape around torn rib cartilage, he dropped to his knees in agony after what was to be the winning throw on his next-to-last attempt.

"I thought my ribs would fall off," he said.

Four years later at Mexico City the thirty-three-year-old Oerter, who later became a computer executive for the Grumman Corporation not far from his West Islip, New York, home, was suffering from a torn muscle high in his right thigh. After his second throw he was in third place. On his next try, he heaved the discus 212-6, the longest throw of his career.

"I love the movement of the toss itself, the purity of it," the two-time world-record holder said. "It's very much like a dancer's motion."

The performance of pole vaulters improved drastically when fiberglass poles replaced bamboo poles, but discus throwers have had to rely on fine-tuning their techniques and increasing their strength. The discus, made of metal and wood and shaped like a saucer, isn't that much different from what it was in the ancient Olympics; the men's discus weighs 4 pounds, 6.5 ounces, the women's discus 2 pounds, 3.25 ounces. In the century since the first modern Olympics, the winning distance in the discus has more than doubled from the winning throw of 95 feet, 7.5 inches in 1896. In addition to practicing his windup and toss, Oerter lifted weights and supplemented his diet of meal bread, fresh vegetables, and brown rice with a drink of raw protein blended with honey, raw eggs, yeast, and orange juice. "The idea," he said, "is to convert strength to throwing power."

Oerter's throwing of a weighty object, like Carl Lewis's running and jumping, evolved from humankind's first sports. Long before the Greeks ran to Marathon, cavemen were running, jumping, and throwing things: running away from preying animals and throwing rocks at them, jumping over logs or bushes. In the twelfth century A.D. some Englishmen set apart a field for running, jumping, and throwing, but it wasn't until 1834 that formal track-and-field meets were organized there. In 1868 the New York Athletic Club was formed, the first in the United States of what are known now as track clubs.

**Al Oerter, in Melbourne, winning
his first of four discus golds**

Wilma Rudolph's "Butterfly" Feeling

Track and field eventually became a popular college sport, not only for men but for women. One of the first women's college track teams was the Tigerbelles of Tennessee State University in Nashville, featuring Wilma Rudolph.

The twentieth of twenty-two children fathered by Ed Rudolph, a railroad porter, in two marriages, four-year-old Wilma was afflicted suddenly and simultaneously with double pneumonia and scarlet fever. Her left leg was paralyzed. Once a week her mother, Blanche, drove her forty-five miles from their Clarksville, Tennessee, home to a Nashville hospital for treatment. By the time she was six she was hopping on one leg; at eight she was walking with a leg brace and then with an orthopedic shoe. Her mother discovered her at eleven playing basketball in her bare feet.

Wilma Rudolph streaked to three gold medals at Rome.

"My father pushed me to be competitive," Rudolph said. "He felt that sports would help me overcome my problems."

Her high school basketball coach, Clinton Gray, nicknamed her Skeeter, short for "mosquito." "You're just like a skeeter," he said. "You're little. You're fast. And you're always in my way." Her coach didn't know how fast. Ed Temple, the Tennessee State coach who ran a summer track camp for girls, developed her into a sixteen-year-old Olympic bronze medalist in the 4 x 100 women's relay in 1956 at Melbourne. Four years later, at Rome, she won three gold medals in the 100, 200, and 4 x 100 relay.

"When I was running," she once said, "I had the sense of freedom, of running in the wind. I never forgot all the years when I was a little girl and not able to be involved in sports. When I ran, I felt like a butterfly. That feeling was always there."

The next year Rudolph was voted the Sullivan Award as America's outstanding amateur athlete. But with track more than two decades short of any moneymaking power for a woman runner, she taught second grade, coached track and basketball, operated a community center, coached at DePauw University in Indiana, had four children in two marriages that ended in divorce, wrote her autobiography, and inspired a prime-time TV movie.

Rudolph has endured as a shining symbol of women's track beyond her 1994 death from a brain tumor.

"Wilma showed that it was okay for a woman to be powerful and black and beautiful," said Benita Fitzgerald-Brown, the 1984 gold medalist in the 100-meter hurdles.

But what Wilma Rudolph accomplished inspired male athletes too. Edwin Moses, arguably the best hurdler in history, has testified to what she meant to him and to others.

"Everybody says Wilma was a great role model for young women track athletes," Moses said, "but she was a hero to all of us in the sport."

Edwin Moses's Thirteen Strides

When Rudolph won her three gold medals, five-year-old Edwin Moses was growing up in Dayton, Ohio, the son of two educators. His father, Irving, was a science teacher and later a principal. His mother, Gladys, was a school supervisor. Quiet and introverted, young Moses applied his studious manner to hurdling. In the 400 hurdles most competitors took fifteen strides between the thirty-six-inch-high barriers; only a few took fourteen. For those who took fifteen, it meant a total of ten extra strides. For those who took fourteen, it meant jumping one hurdle with your right leg forward, the next hurdle with your left leg forward.

"I decided to take thirteen strides," Moses said. "I was told it was impossible, that I couldn't do it, that no one could do it."

At a long-legged six-two he did it. He won the 400 hurdles gold medal at Montreal in 1976, and after losing to West Germany's Harald Schmid on August 27, 1977, he had a streak of 122 consecutive victories in the 400 hurdles (107 in finals, another 15 in preliminaries) until he was nipped by Danny Harris in a Madrid meet on June 4, 1987—a streak that lasted nine years, nine months, and nine days. The streak included his second gold medal, at Los Angeles in 1984.

"It took me two years," Moses said in alluding to his first gold medal, "to realize that when they put the flag up there at Montreal, it wasn't only for me. I also represented 220 million other people."

Edwin Moses hurdles to the 400 gold at Los Angeles.

Mary Decker Slaney's Struggle

Mary Decker Slaney, who fell in a tangle with Zola Budd in the 1984 Olympics at Los Angeles, never got a gold medal. But that shouldn't detract from what she accomplished as America's best woman distance runner. For setting world records in seven events from 800 meters to 10,000 meters in 1982, she was voted the Sullivan Award as the nation's outstanding amateur athlete.

"I really love to train and love to run," she said. "I don't say I *have* to run. I say, hey, I *get* to run today. I don't have to be pushed. I have to be held back."

Sprinters and middle-distance runners require explosive bursts of speed over a relatively short distance, but distance runners need stamina. At a slender five-six and 110 pounds, Slaney ran twice a day, except Sunday, for a total of six to ten miles daily, usually at a six-

Mary Decker Slaney sprawls after tripping in a tangle with barefoot Zola Budd at Los Angeles.

minute-mile pace. After surgery to repair shin splints and a torn Achilles tendon, she never ran more than a total of sixty miles in any one week. But after each workout she also did sit-ups, push-ups, and leg lifts.

"Generally, the track world breaks down into form runners and strength runners," said Frank Shorter, the 1972 Olympic marathon champion. "Mary is a remarkable combination of form and strength."

As a sixth grader in Los Angeles she spotted a bulletin board notice for a cross-country meet. She didn't even know what *cross-country* meant, but she entered. And won. She entered a county meet. And won. She entered a state meet. And won. At fourteen she set a world record in the 1,000-meter run. At sixteen she set a world record in the 800.

"I honestly think of running as an art form," Mary Decker Slaney has said. "Watching a great race is like looking at a pretty picture. But running is also something that requires total dedication."

Cartwheels and Courage

IN THE SOMERSAULT OF HER VAULT SHE LANDED AS FIRMLY as a seagull on a beach. On the balance beam she clung as surely as a squirrel would. On the uneven bars she whirled as easily as a sparrow fluttering from branch to branch in a tall tree. In her floor exercises she was part ballerina, part cheerleader.

With her dark pigtails tied with red and white yarn, fourteen-year-old Nadia Comaneci of Romania dazzled the world at the 1976 Summer Games in Montreal.

Until then no gymnast, male or female, had ever recorded a perfect 10, but this eighty-six-pound European was awarded a 10 seven times by the Olympic judges. In her quiet poise she never blinked.

"If it was perfect," she said of her performance, "I deserved a ten."

At Montreal she won three gold medals (all-around, uneven bars, and balance beam). At the 1980 Summer Games in Moscow she added two more golds and a silver. When the woman whose name is pronounced ko-ma-NEECH stopped competing in 1983, she had earned twenty-one gold medals in Olympic and world championship competition.

"Nadia," said her Romanian coach, Bela Karolyi, who later defected to America, "was a monument of the aggressive type of competitor. If you're a timid scaredy-type person, a little scared puppy dog, you cannot do this."

Karolyi, who operated a gymnastics school in Onesti, Romania, was searching the local elementary schools for more students in 1968, when he spotted two six-year-old girls doing cartwheels in the corner of their school yard during recess. Just then the school

Gymnastics' perfect 10, Nadia Comaneci, struts her stuff at Montreal.

bell rang. The two little girls disappeared into their classroom.

"I hadn't been close enough to see their faces," Karolyi recalled. "I went from classroom to classroom, asking the kids, 'Who likes gymnastics?' They didn't know what the word meant. I asked, 'Who likes to do cartwheels?' Some of the kids raised their hands, and I had them do cartwheels, but none of the kids were the two I had seen."

In the last classroom Karolyi asked if the kids could do cartwheels. Two little girls nodded. Karolyi asked each to do one.

"You're the girls I saw doing cartwheels in the corner of the school yard," Karolyi said. "What are your names?"

One girl answered, "Viorica Dumitru." The other said, "Nadia Comaneci." Karolyi invited them to his gymnastics school, if their parents approved. Soon the two little six-year-olds were training with weights and ropes, running and jumping. In their makeshift gym Karolyi set up two balance beams by stretching a piece of wood across two boxes, then taught the girls how to do walkovers and cartwheels on them.

Three months later Karolyi had his students compete for trophies and gifts. The best gymnast that day was Viorica, but Nadia had a trait that appealed to her coach.

"Nadia never said, 'No,' or 'I can't do that,'" Karolyi writes in his autobiography, *Feel No Fear*. "It didn't matter what the stunt was, how difficult or frightening, she was always ready to perform. That enabled her to progress rapidly."

In three years nine-year-old Nadia Comaneci was the Romanian junior champion; at eleven she was the Romanian national champion; at thirteen, in 1975, she was the youngest to win the European championship, her springboard to Olympic triumph. But it had taken time. As with any other eventual Olympic champion, at first she learned by her mistakes.

"It is difficult to tell with children who are nine, ten and eleven, who will become a champion," Karolyi writes: "You can tell how flexible they are, how coordinated, but not if they have the spirit or if they can develop the mental and physical discipline necessary."

That necessary spirit was evident to Karolyi when Comaneci won the Romanian junior championship. During the competition she fell off the balance beam three times. In her eagerness to climb back on it, she fell off the other side. She wasn't discouraged or defeated by having fallen off. She wanted to win in a sport that a seventeen-year-old Soviet pixie had put onto the world's television stage at the 1972 Summer Games in Munich.

Olga Korbut's Excitement

In her red leotards and with red bows in her pigtails, Olga Korbut, from the city of Grodno in Byelorussia, won two gold medals, in floor exercises and the balance beam.

"Olga was explosive," Karolyi has said. "Her temperament, her personality. She brought to gymnastics the excitement of performing. She was so positive."

In competitions decided by subjective judging, especially that of the international panel used in the Olympics and the world championships, Korbut projected the four elements that impress the judges: difficulty of the performance, gymnast's enjoyment of it, gymnast's artistic manner, crowd influence.

"The judges," Karolyi once said, "don't go against the crowd."

Until Korbut captivated the ABC television cameras, gymnastics had been a relatively obscure

Olga Korbut put gymnastics on worldwide television at Munich.

Olympic sport. The word is derived from the ancient Greek, meaning "athletic or disciplinary exercises." In the United States a men's national championship was first held in 1897; at the 1904 Summer Games in St. Louis, two Americans, Anton Heida and George Eyser, won two gold medals.

The Olympics included women's gymnastics in 1928, but Europeans and an occasional Asian dominated until 1984, when the U.S. men's team outscored China's world champions and Mary Lou Retton won the women's all-around gold. To win the gold medal, the U.S. men had to perform almost perfectly in their last routine, the high bar. Their coach, Abe Grossfeld, thought it might be best for his gymnasts to be conservative, thereby assuring themselves of points with virtually safe moves instead of risking the loss of points with dangerous moves. That's when Jim Hartung walked over to his American teammate Peter Vidmar.

"This is the Olympics," Hartung said. "Let's all go for it."

Tim Daggett's Perfect 10

With that feeling, each went for the gold medal, and each got one as a member of the championship team: Hartung, Vidmar, Bart Conner, Mitch Gaylord, Tim Daggett, and Scott Johnson. In the individual championships Vidmar got a gold for the pommel horse, Conner for the parallel bars.

"Now we've proved that we're at the level of China and Russia," Conner said. "Nobody's going to blow us away."

One of those U.S. gold medalists, Tim Daggett, remembered having watched the 1972 Summer Games at Munich, where the Japanese and Russians dominated the gymnastic competition.

"They were what I wanted to be," Daggett said, "but I didn't know if I could get to that level."

One reason at the time was that since 1932 an American gymnast had never won an Olympic medal. But when Peter Korman earned a bronze medal for the United States in the floor exercises in 1976 at Montreal, Daggett was inspired. Then a fourteen-year-old gymnast in

West Springfield, Massachusetts, he soared and flipped for hours on his backyard trampoline, parallel bars, high bars, pommel horse, and tumbling mats.

As a UCLA freshman four years later Daggett thrived on Coach Makoto ("Mako") Sakamoto's strenuous training regimen that, unless

Peter Vidmar riding the pommel horse to a perfect 10 at Los Angeles

he was seriously injured, began with a mile run each day, rain or shine.

"No matter what the weather, no matter how I felt, no matter what else I had to do," he writes in his autobiography, *Dare to Dream*, "the value was the knowledge that it was one more thing I'd done that maybe the others had not."

As the 1984 Olympics approached, Daggett and Vidmar often worked out together under Coach Sakamoto's watchful eye for an hour or two after the other team members had departed the UCLA gym.

"In a competition," Daggett recalls, "the biggest number of routines that a gymnast performs is six in one day. During one week shortly before the Olympics, we scheduled 36 routines in a day."

As the team medal competition between the United States and the reigning world champion, China, came down to the last event, the high bar, Daggett was the next-to-last American to perform.

"I exploded into my routine, cutting through the air with new found power, knowing that when I did my release skills that I was still part of the bar, still connected to its strength. Backward. Forward. Bail through the bottom. Swing from the top. I let go of the bar for my dismount. I heard the bar vibrate with success. 'Stick it, stick it,' I commanded my legs. Then I stuck that dismount cold."

Daggett's perfect 10 had clinched the gold medal for the U.S. men's team. But three years later he twice reminded the world how dangerous gymnastics can be.

Early in 1987, during a workout on the high bar, Daggett landed on his head, rupturing a disk in his back. He soon recovered. Then at the world championships later that year in Rotterdam, Holland, he sprinted down the runway for the vault and soared high into the air.

"Further from the vault, more thrilling than ever before," he recalls. "But somehow I got a little bit crooked in the air, came down a little bit off and, upon impact, heard what sounded like a rifle shot."

The rifle shot was his left leg breaking; an artery also was severed. In addition to needing the bone reset, Daggett required skin graft surgery to smooth the scar on the outside of his left shin. He never competed again. But he will always be remembered for his contribution to the men's gold medal in 1984.

Mary Lou Retton's Devotion

At Los Angeles, another Karolyi pupil, Mary Lou Retton, popularized gymnastics in America even more than the men's team did.

Out of Fairmont, West Virginia, Retton in 1981 was an A student with pierced ears and size-three shoes—and tremendous raw gymnastics talent. By then Karolyi, after having coached fourteen girls to Olympic medals, had defected to the United States with his wife, Marta, and one suitcase, leaving his Mercedes behind. In organizing the Sundance Athletic Club in Houston, he showed how a male gym-

Mary Lou Retton and her coach, Bela Karolyi, celebrate at Los Angeles.

nastics coach often seems to emerge, sometimes controversially, as a father figure for the young girls under his tutelage. He scolds them, and he hugs them.

"Bela's girls were prepared," Retton said after competing against Karolyi's team. "He had them psyched up. They were there with such obvious self-confidence. His whole body says, 'C'mon, let's go.'"

Retton's father, Ronnie, once a teammate of basketball Hall of Famer Jerry West at West Virginia University, operated a coal industry equipment business. With her parents' permission, Retton moved to Houston early in 1983 to polish her talent under Karolyi's tutelage.

"We had two workouts a day, one at eight in the morning and another at six in the evening," Retton said. "If you missed even one day, you noticed it. Monday was our day off. We had only one workout then."

Retton developed quickly. When the Soviets boycotted the 1984 Summer Games, she emerged as America's sweetheart, winning five medals: a gold in the all-around, silvers in the vault and the team, bronzes in the uneven bars and the floor exercises.

"If you're a gymnast," she once explained, "someone should be able to sneak up and drag you out of bed at midnight and push you out on some strange floor, and you should be able to do your entire routine sound asleep in your pajamas. Without one mistake."

Retton quickly turned her Olympic medals into cash. She earned several million dollars from a fast-food chain; from companies selling cereal, cosmetics, and batteries; from exercise videos; and from her autobiography.

Nadia Comaneci also had her rewards. As perhaps the most famous Romanian in history ("Maybe even more famous than Dracula," some joked) she lived in relative luxury in an eight-room villa with her mother, her brother, and several servants. She drove a Dacia, the best Romanian car. Unlike most Romanians, she was allowed to buy fresh meat, vegetables, and fruit at special stores for the privileged.

But at fifteen, the year after her Montreal triumphs, she had tried to commit suicide. She also had escaped from what turned into an unpleasant romance with Romania's crown prince, Nicu Ceauşescu.

On November 27, 1989, a friend who was living in Hallandale, Florida, thirty-eight-year-old Konstantin Panit, rented an Audi and drove Nadia, then twenty-seven, and six others from Bucharest to a lonely road ten miles from the Hungarian border. At midnight Nadia and the six others began walking through the darkness of the open countryside.

"We were stumbling," she later said. "We often crawled through water and ice."

Hours later they heard watchdogs barking as they hurried through a hole in a barbed-wire fence not far from the Hungarian town of Mezögyan. They had defected. Not far away Panit was waiting for them. Nadia soon was in Austria, and within hours, she had arrived at JFK Airport in New York City.

"I like life," Nadia Comaneci explained. "I want to have a free life."

Spoken with the spirit of the gymnast she was, the gymnast she will always be.

Mark of Excellence

MARK SPITZ HAD ALREADY ACCOMPLISHED WHAT NO other Olympic swimmer ever had, winning five gold medals in the same Summer Games. But now, in 1972 at Munich, he had two days to rest and worry that he might not win the 100-meter freestyle. With his teammate Jerry Heidenreich in top form, he thought about withdrawing to keep his perfect record.

"But if you do that," his longtime coach, Sherman Chavoor, told him, "you'll be a cheese champion."

Mark Spitz swam and won his sixth gold medal; Heidenreich took the silver, half a second behind. The next day the handsome twenty-two-year-old Californian with the black mustache and tousled black hair swam the anchor leg on the U.S. 4 x 100 medley relay team for his seventh gold. Soon he was posing for a poster with the seven gold medals draped artistically around his neck.

"They're heavy," he said.

Those seven gold medals were not as heavy as the weight of all those years of swimming in lonely pools at dawn, of having bragged that he would win six gold medals at Mexico City in 1968 and winning only two, in relays. They were not as heavy as would be the weight of his hoping to capitalize on his Olympic theatrics by trying to be an actor.

"Everybody wanted me to be special—'When's your next movie? When's your next TV show?'" he said a decade later. "Just because I was a good swimmer, in America they expect you to be a star. But I turned down movie offers because I won't do something if I can't do it well."

As if cheering himself on, Mark Spitz splashes in the 200 butterfly at Munich.

What he did well was swim in the Olympics, as no one before or since ever has. As a youngster in Walnut Creek, California, he got up at five A.M. with his mother, Lenore, who drove him forty miles to Santa Clara to train. His father, Arnold, soon moved the family to Santa Clara and took another job as the operations manager of a scrap metal company in Oakland, to ease his son's travel time.

"There was a point where I pushed him, I guess," Arnold Spitz once said, "but if I hadn't pushed my son, he never would have been at Santa Clara. Swimming isn't everything. Winning is."

After Mark Spitz's disappointment at Mexico City, when some of his Olympic teammates taunted him for his arrogance, he enrolled as a predental student at Indiana University, where the legendary James ("Doc") Counsilman was the swimming coach.

"Mark prided himself on not training too hard," Counsilman said, "but it was easy to psych him into workouts. I just bet him a milk shake he couldn't do it."

Prior to the 1992 Summer Games at Barcelona, just about everybody was telling Spitz that he couldn't do it, that he couldn't possibly qualify at age forty-two for the U.S. Olympic team. He wasn't hoping to win seven medals again, only the gold in the 100-meter butterfly. He was a real estate developer now. He had lost twenty-five pounds and had shaved off his mustache long ago. He was hoping to be the oldest swimmer to win an Olympic medal; the oldest had been Duke Kahanamoku, the Hawaiian who won the 100 freestyle gold for the United States in 1920 at age thirty and the 100 freestyle silver in 1924 at age thirty-four.

"I am probably in the best shape cardiovascular-wise and physically than anybody my age," Spitz insisted. "I don't care what sport you're talking about."

However good his condition, it wasn't good enough. He lost a match race in the 50 butterfly by 1.78 seconds, a lifetime in swimming. He simply was no longer capable of competing on the Olympic level.

Swimming is believed to have originated when prehistoric humans watched animals paddle in a lake or river. But the competitive sport as we know it now is believed to have originated in England around the turn of the nineteenth century. Indoor pools were built for swimmers using the breaststroke. At a London meet in 1844 several Native Americans, their arms thrashing the water, introduced the crawl, now known as the freestyle. The backstroke and butterfly stroke were to provide a total of four Olympic strokes. Over the last century Olympic and world records have improved dramatically as a result of better coaching, better training, better conditioning. At the 1896 Summer Olympics, for example, the winning time in the men's 100 freestyle was 1 minute, 22.2 seconds; in 1992 it was 49.02 seconds, a drop of 33 seconds.

"The great ones do everything right, naturally," Counsilman said. "They have a feel for the water. Subconsciously they are seeking the greatest resistance in the water. They feel it in their palms, on their shoulders and heads. The great ones know when their stroke is right."

Tracy Caulkins's Forty-eight Titles

One of the great ones was Tracy Caulkins, a tall Tennessean who won a record forty-eight national titles in all four strokes and set fifty-eight national women's records. Voted the 1978 Sullivan Award at age fifteen as the nation's outstanding amateur athlete, she was the youngest ever accorded that honor. Before the boycott of the 1980 Summer Games she was favored to win five gold medals in Moscow, but she had to wait until 1984 to earn three golds: the 200 and 400 individual medleys and the 4 x 100 medley relay. She never complained.

Tracy Caulkins earned three golds at Los Angeles.

"Tracy is like an actress who's in it for the theater, not to be a star," her teammate Nancy Hogshead said. "Tracy is in swimming for the competition, not for the headlines."

As skilled as Olympic champions are, not all enjoy the long, tiring hours of training, the exile from the everyday fun of their teenage years. But whining was never Caulkins's style.

While training at the Nashville Aquatic Club, she often swam anywhere from ten thousand to twenty thousand yards a day. That's roughly two to four miles at intervals of fifty to eight hundred yards.

"Tracy has an amazing ability to hold on to the water," one of her coaches, Bob Munoz, once said. "When a swimmer is efficient, her hand is always searching for water that's not moving, finding it, using it. That's a gift. I don't think you can teach that."

Because of her versatility, Caulkins's workout often included three 50-yard butterflies, one 150-yard easy individual medley, three 50-yard backstrokes, another 150-yard individual medley, three 50-yard breaststrokes, another 150-yard individual medley, and three 50-yard freestyles. She concluded with another 150-yard individual medley.

"In the water I can sense where the other swimmers are and how they're doing because we're all in it together," she said. "It's like we're touching, in a way. I know a lot of people think it's monotonous down the black lines over and over, but it's not monotonous if you're enjoying what you're doing with forty others who are enjoying it."

Janet Evans's Happiness

Janet Evans enjoyed it too, until she realized she was a target for all the younger swimmers after she had won four gold medals in 1988 and 1992.

"Sometimes I look at the trophies and things from my first years, and it boggles my mind," she said. "It was really fun then, but it didn't always stay fun. It's harder to stay on top than to get there. Once you're there, you're the one they're aiming for."

Evans's workouts consisted of two hours in the morning (a 1,500-meter warm-up, 500 meters of kicking, 2,000 meters of pulling, and eight 500-meter repeats), then two hours of the same in the afternoon. Six days a week every week. No excuses.

"I've learned a lot since I was fourteen," Evans said as the Summer Games at Atlanta approached. "The biggest thing is that this is just a sport, and what counts isn't winning or losing, but being happy."

The Diving Doctor

Happiness for Sammy Lee was diving. Born in 1920 to Korean immigrant parents in Los Angeles, he bristled at racial taunts that made him all the more determined to succeed not only as a doctor but as a diver. As a premedical student at UCLA, he was warned that his diving workouts were distracting him from his medical studies.

"You can't do both," one of his advisers said. "If you don't concentrate on your college work, I won't recommend you for medical school."

Lee kept diving, but he also kept studying. He graduated from the University of Southern California medical school as an eye, ear, nose, and throat specialist, then entered the U.S. Army as a lieutenant during the closing months of World War II. At the 1948 Summer Games in London he won the platform diving gold medal. In 1952 at Helsinki he won again, at thirty-two the oldest diver ever to win a gold medal.

Diving, one of the most artistic Olympic sports, is believed to have begun in the seventeenth century, when Swedish and German gymnasts performed at beaches in the summer on equipment perched over water. By the late nineteenth century "plunging" meets were held in England. In 1893 the Royal Life Saving Society of Great Britain organized what was known as a graceful diving competition. In 1904 the Olympics added diving.

Greg Louganis's Sanctuary

More than seven decades later, as one of Greg Louganis's early coaches, Dr. Sammy Lee helped develop the best diver in history. And like his coach, Louganis had to endure taunts.

Born of a Samoan fisherman and a northern European mother in

With a bandage on his head, Greg Louganis springs to the gold medal at Seoul.

San Diego, the infant was adopted at nine months by a bookkeeper, Peter Louganis, and his wife, Frances. At age six he could tap-dance. At ten he excelled in gymnastics as well as in diving. But because his biological father was a Samoan, some of his schoolmates called him "nigger." When he found reading difficult because of what was diagnosed later as dyslexia, he was called "retard." But at the diving pool nobody taunted him.

"The pool was my sanctuary," he said.

The pool was also his waterway to Olympic glory. At age sixteen in the 1976 Summer Games at Montreal he took the platform silver medal. By 1979 he was considered the world's best diver, but the United States boycott of the 1980 Games in Moscow kept him off that year's Olympic stage. In 1984 he swept both golds.

"People talk about tens; in one meet Greg had thirty-five or forty of them," his longtime coach, Ron O'Brien, said. "In his career he's probably had two hundred."

Only five-nine and 160 pounds, Louganis soared, spun, and slid into the water with hardly a ripple. Time after time. But in a qualifying dive in the preliminary round at Seoul, his forehead slapped the springboard, a moment that haunted him seven years later.

"I was so embarrassed I wanted to disappear," he said after qualifying with ease despite four surgical stitches in his bloodied forehead. "But I think it made me concentrate better the next time."

When Louganis, who publicly acknowledged his homosexuality at the 1994 Gay Games, disclosed early in 1995 that he had AIDS and had known in 1988 that he had the HIV virus when he competed in Seoul, that bloodied forehead surfaced as a medical issue. His blood had been in the pool. Even though he thought that the chlorine in the diving pool's water would dilute whatever blood he lost, he knew that AIDS can be transmitted to others through blood.

"I thought there was not too much of a chance, you know, because it takes a while if you cut yourself on the head; usually it takes a minute to start bleeding," Louganis said. "And there is chlorine in the pool all over; the deck's wet with chlorinated water."

After the accident a doctor stitched Louganis's two-inch cut without wearing protective gloves. That doctor, Dr. James Puffer, the chief physician for the 1988 U.S. Olympic team, didn't know that Louganis had been HIV positive in 1988 until Louganis informed him early in 1994. Puffer had himself tested the next day; the test was negative.

"Do I say something?" Louganis said, alluding to his 1988 decision not to inform USOC officials. "It's...you know, this has been an incredibly guarded secret."

At the time of Louganis's disclosure that he had AIDS, the USOC made voluntary testing available to its athletes but, like many other sports organizations, did not require athletes who are HIV positive to announce that they are infected.

Other than Louganis, the only other person aware of the diver's being HIV positive at Seoul was Ron O'Brien, his coach. At the time O'Brien agreed with Louganis's decision to be quiet. "If it were in a sport like boxing or wrestling, football, where there's a lot of contact, personal contact," O'Brien said, "I would have been very concerned. But our sport is such that you don't ever come close to anybody."

As a diver Greg Louganis was certainly never close to anybody. Slicing into the pool with hardly a splash, in 1984 he won the two diving gold medals at Los Angeles; in 1988 he won the two diving gold medals at Seoul. Over two Olympics he won all four golds.

No diver had ever done that before. No diver may ever do it again.

Figure Skating

Ballet on Ice

WALKING ON THE STREET, HAVING DINNER IN A restaurant, or figure skating on the ice, Katarina Witt enjoys being noticed.

"It doesn't matter where I am," the two-time Olympic champion has said. "If I feel eyes on me, I am better."

Few, if any, figure skaters have ever been better. While representing East Germany, Witt won the gold medal at Sarajevo in 1984 and another gold medal at Calgary in 1988 before joining a touring ice show. When professional skaters were ruled eligible for the Winter Games at Lillehammer in 1994, she returned to Olympic competition.

In her long program there she wore a blood-red costume and skated to the antiwar song "Where Have All the Flowers Gone?," her "message for peace" in bombed and battered Sarajevo.

At the age of twenty-eight, advanced for a figure skater, Witt finished seventh, far behind the Olympic champion, Oksana Baiul of Ukraine, but the dazzling German brunette was applauded as if she had won a third gold medal. She took that to mean that the six thousand people in the arena had understood her message about Sarajevo, where she had won her first gold medal a decade earlier.

"I know this is maybe naive," she said later, "but one day I hope there will be peace in the world. Maybe one day the flowers will come back."

Witt's feeling for flowers is only natural. Flowers are almost as much a part of women's figure skating as the ice itself. After a figure skating competition, just as a ballerina is handed a bouquet of

Two-time gold medalist Katarina Witt enjoys the world's eyes on her.

flowers during a curtain call, a figure skater is handed a bouquet of flowers by her coach or her family.

The connection is understandable. More than anything else, figure skating is ballet on ice. For men as well as women.

John Curry's Milestone

Perhaps the most elegant figure skater of all, John Curry, the Englishman who won the 1976 men's gold medal, grew up wanting to be a ballet dancer before his father smothered that ambition. Turning to skating, he eventually was described by many experts as the Nureyev of figure skating, a reference to Rudolph Nureyev, perhaps the most artistic ballet dancer of all.

"John represented a milestone in skating," his coach, Carlo Fassi, said after Curry's death from AIDS at age forty-four. "He completely changed skating, turning it into a real art."

After winning his Olympic gold medal at Innsbruck, Curry starred in his *Ice Dancing* show at a New York theater in 1977 and later toured with his John Curry Skating Company. But his performances were always more artistic than show biz.

"I never could see the point," he once said, "of spending twelve years training to go dress up in a Bugs Bunny suit. I was brought up on the Royal Ballet, and I hope it shows in my work."

Figure skating is a sport with balletlike jumps and spins on concave steel blades that cut through the ice. The blades' two sharp edges need to be sharpened constantly. The skates have an outside edge on the outside of the foot and an inside edge toward the body; each edge has a front and a back. Different jumps and moves are made from the specific edges. There are two basic types of jumps: edge jumps and toe jumps.

In the Olympics four events are held: women's singles, men's singles, pairs, and ice dancing.

In singles and pairs the competition is split into a short program and a long program. In the short program of two and one-half minutes (which counts for one-third of the scoring) the skaters are required to perform certain jumps and spins. In the long, or freestyle, program of four and one-half minutes (which counts for two-thirds of the scoring) the skater is marked on creativity and skill.

Pairs skating is more athletic but less artistic than ice dancing, in which skaters are not allowed to do spins; they also are not allowed to skate apart from their partners. The ice dancing competition consists of two compulsory dances, an original dance, and a free dance.

The judges award two marks, one for artistic impression, the other for technical merit. The highest possible mark is 6.0; there are mandatory deductions for certain mistakes, but subjective judgment is usually a factor. If a tie in the scoring develops, the tiebreaker is the higher score of the technical merit in the short program and the higher score for artistic impression in the long program.

The jumps are named after the skaters who first performed them: the triple axel (for Axel Paulsen of Norway), the salchow (for Ulrich Salchow of Sweden), the lutz (for Alois Lutz of Austria).

Of all the jumps, the triple axel is the easiest to understand. It starts when the skater glides forward on one skate, leaps into the air, rotates three and one-half times, then lands on the opposite foot, skating backward.

The salchow involves a wide leg swing, which creates rotation at the liftoff. While moving backward, the skater jumps off one foot and does one, two, or three full turns in the air, then lands on the opposite foot, skating backward.

In the lutz the skater usually moves forward in a long, sweeping curve, takes off from the left back outside edge while assisted by the right toe, then turns counterclockwise and lands on the outside back edge of the right foot.

Of all the Olympic sports, women's figure skating invariably attracts the highest television ratings in America as well as throughout much of the world.

Oksana Baiul Arrives

In the 1994 Winter Games at Lillehammer, the primary figure skating plot involved Nancy Kerrigan's silver medal on a knee damaged by Tonya Harding's hired muggers. In the confusion Oksana Baiul, a sixteen-year-old skater from Ukraine, once part of the Soviet Union, soared to the gold medal after having won the world championship the year before. As a little girl whose divorced father left when she was two, Baiul was allowed to skate by her mother and grandfather only to keep her fit until she could begin ballet lessons at age seven.

"But when I was seven," she has said, "I won my first competition, so I decided to stay in figure skating."

Her grandfather died in 1987, when she was ten; her grandmother died the next year. In 1991 her mother died. Although her father attended her mother's funeral, she considered him a stranger.

"Oksana didn't know him," her coach then, Stanislav Koritek, said. "Really, she had no father, no family."

Soon she had no coach. Koritek moved to Canada in 1991 to tutor skaters, leaving Baiul alone. But his father phoned Galina Zmievskaya, a coach in Odessa who had developed Viktor Petrenko, who was to be the 1992 Olympic champion. With two daughters of her own, Zmievskaya was understandably concerned about the financial commitment, but Petrenko persuaded her to take in the teenager from Ukraine.

"She is only one girl," Petrenko said. "How much can she cost?"

Petrenko bought Baiul's skates and costumes, then married Zmievskaya's oldest daughter, easing the coach's household expenses. Baiul's quick development soon eased any other concerns her coach may have had. At age fifteen, not much bigger than a long-stemmed rose at five-three and ninety-five pounds, she emerged as not only the youngest world champion since Sonja Henie but a purist.

"Women should stop trying to be like men with the jumps," she has said. "People forget that the beauty is the key. The most important thing is the skating."

Figure skating didn't develop until 1863 in Vienna, Austria, when

Oksana Baiul, the gold-medal winner at Lillehammer

Jackson Haines, a visiting American ballet master, suggested that music be played while people were ice skating. Soon the idea spread to Canada and then to the United States. It was included in the Summer Games as early as 1908, long before the first Winter Games in 1924, but it wasn't glamorized until Norway's Sonja Henie won three consecutive gold medals and ten consecutive world championships before emerging as a motion-picture star and ice show impresario.

Henie's style on the ice helped pave the way for the popular success she later enjoyed. She wore short skirts, ermine-trimmed satin costumes, and white skates; her rivals wore frumpy black skates.

Dick Button's Perfection

The first American figure skater to win an Olympic gold medal was Dick Button, once scorned by an instructor as "too fat." At the time he was twelve years old, only five-two but 160 pounds. His parents found another coach near their Englewood, New Jersey, home, the young skater lost weight, and at sixteen he won his first of seven consecutive U.S. titles.

"With Dick," his coach, Gus Lussi, said, "nothing short of perfection will satisfy him."

Button won his first Olympic gold medal at St. Moritz in 1948; in 1952 at Oslo he won again.

"My skating was athletic. I changed the style," Button has said. "It was really an American style.

Kristi Yamaguchi glides to the gold at Albertville.

Brash. It was the beginning of a ten-year period in which Americans dominated the sport."

Button graduated from Harvard and Harvard Law School, then signed a $150,000 contract with the Ice Capades. He has since been a prosperous lawyer, businessman, and television show packager, as well as an insightful figure skating television analyst of other Americans who followed him to the Olympics.

Hayes Alan Jenkins and Tenley Albright, the first American woman gold medalist in figure skating, produced the first American sweep at Cortina d'Ampezzo in 1956. David Jenkins, a younger brother of Hayes, and Carol Heiss swept the 1960 golds at Squaw Valley.

Peggy Fleming's Tender Style

In 1961 the entire U.S. figure skating team was wiped out in an airplane crash near Brussels, Belgium. In all, seventy-three skaters, coaches, and officials died. Then in 1964, a flowerlike fifteen-year-old, Peggy Fleming, skated in the Olympics, and at Grenoble in 1968 she won a gold medal, delivering a message to the world that America was still capable of producing Olympic champions.

"I didn't have anyone to look up to and guide my training," Fleming said, "but that was good in a way. To try to copy someone is never a good thing. Being the first of the skaters to do well after the crash definitely helped my career. There were a lot of special feelings when I won, feelings that I was more than just another champion, that I was the first to rise above the tragedy."

Fleming had a tender style polished by her coach, Carlo Fassi, in Colorado Springs, Colorado, after her father, a newspaper pressman, had settled there so she could develop her talent.

"Peggy is a delicate lady on the ice," Dick Button once said. "She is not a fiery skater, and she shouldn't be made to be. With some skaters, there is a lot of fuss and feathers but nothing is happening. With Peggy, there's no fuss and feathers, but a great deal is happening."

In 1964 Fleming won the first of five consecutive United States championships, but a few weeks later at the Winter Games in Innsbruck, she finished sixth. She felt she had done well, but on her return some of her schoolmates complained, "You didn't win a medal." That hurt.

"I think," she said later, "that I really grew up as a result."

Four other American skaters have earned Olympic gold medals: Dorothy Hamill, with her short and sassy hairdo, at Innsbruck in 1976, Scott Hamilton at Sarajevo in 1984, Brian Boitano at Calgary in 1988 in a dramatic duel with Canada's Brian Orser, and Kristi Yamaguchi at Albertville in 1992.

"From the first time I skated when I was six years old," Yamaguchi, who grew up in California, said with a smile, "I visualized winning this gold medal."

Of all the world's figure skaters, perhaps none have been more appealing than Great Britain's ice dancing couple of Jayne Torvill and Christopher Dean. They hypnotized the world with their interpretation of Ravel's *Bolero* in winning the 1984 gold medal at Sarajevo.

"It is passion in a different way than romance," Dean explained. "It's a passion of wanting to do your best, of wanting to bring out what's inside."

Of all the definitions of figure skating through the years, maybe that is the best. But sometimes that passion turned into romance, as it did for Ekaterina Gordeeva and Sergei Grinkov, the Russians who took the pairs gold medal at Calgary in 1988 and at Lillehammer in 1994. They had skated together since 1982, when she was eleven and he was fifteen. They were married in 1991. The next year their daughter, Daria, was born. During a training session in Lake Placid in 1995, Grinkov suddenly slumped to the ice, dead from a heart attack.

"The perfect pair," Dick Button said. "They had everything. He was the perfect husband. They had the perfect career, the perfect marriage."

But as the beautiful twenty-four-year-old widow known as Katia said before her husband's funeral in Moscow, "Maybe everything was too good, too perfect. That was why it could not last."

Legs locked, Jayne Torvill and Christopher Dean whirl to the ice-dancing gold at Sarajevo.

Down the Mountains

TOMMY MOE LEARNED TO SKI THE HARD WAY. WHEN HE was thirteen years old, he was kicked off his Whitefish, Montana, school team for smoking marijuana.

"I was experimenting," he recalled at the 1994 Winter Games in Lillehammer, Norway. "I was a normal kid trying to have a good time."

At the time his parents were divorced and he was living with his mother. But when his father, Tom Moe, Sr., a steel contractor who had moved to Alaska, learned of the marijuana incident, he summoned his son to live with him. Three years later Tommy was caught smoking marijuana again. This time his father wouldn't let him go to South America that summer to ski with some of his buddies.

"You're coming with me," his father said. "To work."

They went to Dutch Harbor in the Aleutian Islands, where he shoveled gravel and crawled in the mud.

"Would you rather do this again next summer?" his father asked him. "Or go skiing in Argentina?"

Tommy Moe got the message.

Six years later he was on the U.S. Olympic team at Albertville, France, where he finished a disappointing twenty-eighth in the giant slalom. Then, in 1994, at Lillehammer he won the Olympic downhill gold medal, only the second American to do so. Billy Johnson, who learned to ski in Boise, Idaho, had been the first, in 1984 at Sarajevo, Yugoslavia. Each stunned the European skiers who consider the Winter Games their private playgrounds.

"I like to beat 'em at their own game," Johnson said of the European skiers. "They think they should always win."

Then again, the Europeans almost always have won. Tommy Moe, Billy Johnson, and Phil Mahre in the 1984 slalom are the only American men to have won a gold medal in Alpine skiing. They joined four American women gold medalists: Andrea Mead Lawrence in both the slalom and the giant slalom in 1952, Gretchen Fraser in the 1948 slalom, Barbara Cochran in the 1972 slalom, and Debbie Armstrong in the 1984 giant slalom.

The sport of skiing originated centuries ago as a means of transportation on snow and ice, sometimes during a war. In the Battle of Oslo in 1200 King Sverre of Sweden equipped his scouts with skis. Late in the sixteenth century skiing spread into Central Europe, notably Austria, and eventually to the United States, Canada, Japan, Australia, New Zealand, and mountainous South American nations.

What is known now as Alpine skiing developed in the Alps Mountains of Switzerland, Austria, France, Italy, and Germany.

Skiing is a much more popular sport in Europe than anywhere else. Several years ago, when France had a population of fifty-six million, it was estimated that half the people skied. And for a skier, the downhill is the most popular and most dangerous race. On television

Ski poles high, Tommy Moe adds a super giant slalom silver medal to his downhill gold at Lillehammer.

the race appears less steep than it really is. Downhill racers swoop down a mountain at speeds up to ninety miles per hour on what is as much ice as snow.

In the slalom, the giant slalom, and the super giant slalom, skiers swerve through a tight series of what are known as gates—pairs of thin, flexible posts with flags atop them. Each is a two-run event.

"You have to race down two separate courses, each with fifty to sixty gates marked by pairs of flagged poles in the snow," Phil and Steve Mahre say in *No Hill Too Fast*, their autobiography. "Each gate demands a precise turn—precise, that is, because one of the secrets to winning a ski race is to travel the shortest distance from the starting gate to the finish line. But it isn't the only secret. Often the shortest distance traveled by the racer is not necessarily the fastest. You have to figure and feel the fastest line down the course. It's a mental juggling act carried on at speeds up to 50 miles an hour over an abrupt span of a minute to a minute and a half."

The Twins' Walkie-talkie

After taking the lead with his second run at Sarajevo in 1984, Phil Mahre spoke over a walkie-talkie to his twin brother, Steve, who was about to go into the starting gate. Onlookers were stunned that a possible gold medalist was helping another skier to beat him.

"For us it was routine," they write. "Each was always trying to help the other do his best, even if it meant being beaten in the process."

Over the walkie-talkie Phil advised Steve to "catch the first six gates with round turns and carry the tempo into the rest of the course. Remember the gate on the knoll where a late turn might cause you to get low? It isn't as bad as it looks. On the bottom face it's slick, so get on and off your edges quickly." Moments later Steve swooped down to the silver medal.

Many of the best Olympic skiers usually learn to ski almost as soon as they learn to walk. Jean-Claude Killy lived in the French village of

Val-d'Isère, which was so high in the Alps he often skied during the summer months. From the windows of Toni Sailer's boyhood home in Kitzbühel, Austria, he could see the cable cars rising to the top of the downhill run known as the Streif.

Killy and Sailer developed into the only two skiers ever to sweep what were then the three Alpine events in the Winter Olympics: downhill, slalom, and giant slalom.

Val-d'Isère, only five miles from the Italian border in the Alps of eastern France, is now a fashionable year-round resort, but when Killy was growing up there, it had no mountain biking trails, no snowboards, no tennis courts.

"I concentrated on skiing," Killy once said. "Skiing was the only way to go beyond the village."

His father, who had been a fighter pilot during World War II with the Free French in Algeria, owned a ski shop in Val-d'Isère and later added a small hotel-restaurant. As a youngster, Jean-Claude skied down the roof of his house. When he went to school, he skied at lunchtime.

"Thursday mornings," he once said, "we were supposed to go to catechism classes, but we skied instead. One day the priest skied out after us in his full robes."

The priest caught Killy that day, but in 1968 in the mountains around Grenoble, France, none of his Olympic rivals caught him. His sweep of the gold medals in the downhill, slalom, and giant slalom provided him with instant fame that he marketed around the world into millions of dollars.

When Sailer was growing up in Kitzbühel, his father was a plumber and a glazier. Toni began to ski when he was two. At six he was skidding down the narrow Streif run, where his father put pine twigs in the snow to create the feeling of the gates in a future downhill or slalom.

As the first to sweep the three Alpine skiing gold medals, at Cortina d'Ampezzo in the Italian Alps in 1956, Sailer emerged as an Austrian idol.

Tall, dark, and handsome, he appeared in movies. He sang. His autobiography was a best-seller. He developed a line of ski clothes. He operated a thirty-two-bed inn on land he received as a gift from Kitzbühel, the town that inspired his nickname, the Blitz from Kitz.

In the Olympics, the Alpine races (which now include super giant slalom and combined, in addition to downhill, slalom, and giant slalom) for men and women are only part of the ski schedule. Nordic skiing has five men's and five women's cross-country events through forests and two men's ski jump events.

Eddie the Eagle

Ski jumpers once soared with their skis parallel, but jumping with skis in a V shape is now the style. Many of the best ski jumpers are teenagers, although Jens Weissflog of Germany won Olympic gold medals ten years apart, at Sarajevo and at Lillehammer.

The most popular ski jumper in Olympic history was also quite likely the worst. Eddie ("The Eagle") Edwards arrived in Calgary in 1988 as Great Britain's best ski jumper...also its only ski jumper.

His skis and his heart aflutter, Eddie ("The Eagle") Edwards soars shakily at Calgary. For Eddie the Eagle, the most important thing was "to survive."

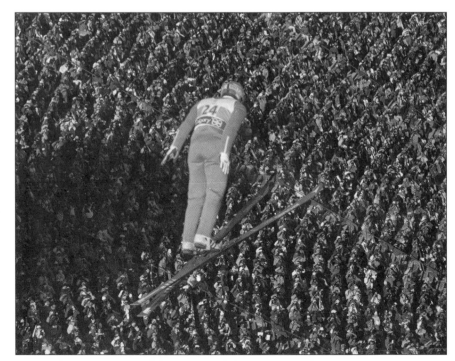

Eddie the Eagle was a skinny reddish-haired twenty-four-year-old plasterer from Cheltenham, England, who squinted through pink glasses. Olympic ski jumpers like to think of what they do as flying, but Eddie the Eagle fluttered. He had to borrow skis from the Austrians, a helmet from the Italians, a ski suit from the Germans. He finished fifty-eighth and last in the 70-meter jump and fifty-fifth and last in the 90-meter jump, wobbling only 180 feet each time. In contrast, Matti Nykänen of Finland soared 294 feet to his 90-meter gold. Even so, Eddie the Eagle was elated.

"The most important thing for me," he said, "was to survive."

He returned to England a national idol. He hired an agent, sold his story to the London *Daily Mail* for sixty-five thousand dollars, and dreamed about a motion-picture career after a conversation with actor Burt Reynolds during an appearance with Johnny Carson on *The Tonight Show.*

"I know I'm just Eddie Edwards, the plasterer, and sport is so professional now," he said. "But haven't I brought something back to Olympic sport? Like, what did they used to call it? Ah, yes, taking part."

Taking part defines the Olympic spirit, but that doesn't mean just anybody can take part. For all the fun Eddie the Eagle created in Calgary, he didn't deserve to take part in the Olympics, especially in such a dangerous event. He would not take part again. Before the 1992 Winter Games at Albertville, the British Olympic Association tightened its qualifying standards to protect Eddie the Eagle and others from themselves. To compete in the Olympics, an athlete should be required to meet a standard for a sense of skill, not a sense of humor.

Lyubov Yegorova's Nine Medals

Cross-country skiing is popular in the Nordic nations of Norway (where 25 percent of the 4.2 million population participates), Sweden, and Finland, as well as in the colder regions of the former Soviet Union and Canada.

"On a good winter Sunday you can see thousands of people out on the tracks around Oslo," said Per Nymoen, the Norwegian Ski Association's organizational director. "It has been so for a hundred years."

Lyubov Yegorova grew up in Siberia hoping to be a ballerina. Instead she developed into a cross-country skier with nine Olympic medals, including six golds. As a member of the Unified Team representing twelve former Soviet republics in 1992, she earned three gold medals and two silvers at Albertville; representing Russia in 1994 at age twenty-seven, she won three more golds and another silver at Lillehammer.

Yegorova's six gold medals matched the individual record total for the Winter Olympics, set by the Soviet speed skater Lydia Skoblikova in 1960 and 1964.

"Everybody talks about records," Yegorova said in Lillehammer, "but I don't care if I beat the record or not. I don't run after records. I simply work."

Through the years only one American has earned an Olympic medal in the Nordic ski events. In the 1976 Winter Games in Innsbruck, nineteen-year-old Bill Koch, out of Guilford, Vermont, took the silver in the 30-kilometer cross-country race even though his breathing was restricted by asthma.

"There's something very spirited about cross-country," he said. "It really moves me. Sometimes I see it as an art form."

Skiing is part of the biathlon, a combination of cross-country skiing and small-bore rifle marksmanship in three events for men and three events for women. Myriam Bedard, a Canadian woman, won both of the women's individual events at Albertville.

Donna Weinbrecht's "Motorcross"

Olympic medals also are awarded for a relatively new sport, freestyle skiing, in moguls (snowy bumps) and aerials.

Freestyle skiing, which originated in the United States in the

1960s as hotdog skiing, requires shorter skis and longer, sturdier poles. But it wasn't recognized as an Olympic sport until 1992, when Donna Weinbrecht's wild ride down dozens of snowy bumps showed how mogul skiing demands the delicate balance of a surfer, the reckless daring of a ski jumper, the thumping rhythm of a disco dancer, and the shock absorbers of an amusement park bumper car.

Donna Weinbrecht bounces to her mogul freestyle gold medal at Albertville.

"I call it the motorcross of winter," she said.

In many sports the system coddles potential Olympic champions. But growing up in West Milford, New Jersey, about thirty miles from New York City, Weinbrecht did it all herself. She worked as a waitress in Killington, Vermont, where her father had constructed a family ski lodge. In 1987 she made the U.S. team; in 1990 she was the World Cup champion.

When she arrived at Albertville in 1992, she was the Olympic favorite in the event she had virtually created.

"The pressure was there. I couldn't fool myself, I was expected to win," she said after earning the gold medal. "My thoughts were on the kids who wrote me letters. To be brave. To be right here and now, not somewhere else. Be in the gate. Be ready to go."

Her philosophy was the same as that of any of the more famous downhill racers or the cross-country competitors or the ski jumpers or the biathletes. No matter what the event, it's on skis. Only the method is different.

Queen and King of Hearts

THE MORNING AFTER THE 1992 WINTER GAMES IN Albertville ended, hundreds of Olympic athletes, coaches, and officials were waiting on long lines at the check-in counters in the Geneva, Switzerland, airport. Many had porters carrying their bulging bags, but little Bonnie Blair, a double gold-medal winner at Albertville, was pushing her own luggage cart.

Typical.

Of all the American women in Olympic history, speed skater Bonnie Blair has won the most gold medals: five. With a total of six medals, including a bronze, she is the United States's most decorated Winter Olympian—surpassing speed skater Eric Heiden's sweep of five golds in 1980 at Lake Placid—but she seems more in awe of other Olympic champions than she is of herself.

"I don't see myself as being up on a podium," she has said, "but I see them that way."

Maybe that's why Bonnie Blair was so successful, as well as so enduring and so endearing.

At Calgary in 1988 she won the 500 and finished third in the 1,000; at Albertville in 1992 she won the 500 and the 1,000; and at Lillehammer in 1994 she repeated in the 500 and the 1,000.

Before each of her races she fortified herself the way little kids do: with a peanut butter and jelly sandwich.

In winning the same event in a record three consecutive Winter Games, Blair was blessed by the rescheduled two-year gap between Albertville and Lillehammer rather than the usual four-year wait. But

no other speed skater won a gold medal in each of her three Winter Games over a six-year span.

"I seem to skate my best in the Olympics," she has said. "It must be something about the Olympics that gets me going a little more."

It's almost as if Blair were destined to be a speed skater. The day she was born in Champaign, Illinois, her father, Charlie, drove her mother, Eleanor, to the hospital. In those years before doctors allowed husbands in the delivery room, he departed to time races at a speed skating meet. With four older brothers and an older sister, the baby of the Blair family grew up as a "tag-along kid," following her siblings everywhere. But in a few years her father was timing her races.

"No matter what the competition, no matter what the training routine," she has said, "I'd try to find a goal within it and try to better it."

At five-four and 130 pounds, Blair aimed to be as strong as possible to cope with her rivals, many of whom were taller and more powerful. Six days a week she ran, cycled, and lifted weights in addition to skating laps.

"We do it because we love what we're doing," she has said. "I never got into it to make money."

Blair's gold medals put her picture on Kellogg's cornflakes boxes in the United States, but she was even more popular in northern Europe, where speed skating is a more popular sport. Before her races at Lillehammer she was serenaded by Dutch fans singing, "My Bonnie Lies over the Ocean," the ultimate compliment from people in the Netherlands, the small nation of frozen canals that took speed skating to its heart centuries ago.

The word *skates* is believed to be a derivation of the Dutch word *schaats*, although historians don't know if the Dutch, Norwegians, Swedes, or Finns first used skates. These early skates were presumably made of bone or wood.

After the development of the iron skate blade in 1572, skating emerged as a sport in Scotland, with the organization of the Skating Club of Edinburgh and other clubs. Scots emigrated to Canada with

Bonnie Blair completes her 500–1,000 double at Albertville.

their skates. Then the sport filtered into the northern United States, where in 1850 a Philadelphia inventor, E. W. Bushnell, created a steel skate blade that revolutionized skating in North America and Europe. Over the years equipment, along with the natural evolution of better training and coaching, has improved performance. The blades on speed skates are much longer than on figure skates or hockey skates in order to permit a longer glide without any loss of speed. In a sport in which medals are decided by tenths and sometimes hundredths of a second, skintight one-piece suits create less air resistance.

Heiden Inspires Koss

Of all the world's speed skaters, none ever dominated a Winter Games as Eric Heiden did in 1980 at Lake Placid by winning all five of the men's events: the 500, 1,000, 1,500, 5,000, and 10,000.

Wearing a gold racing suit that later was displayed in the Smithsonian Institution in Washington, D.C., Heiden emerged as the world's most famous athlete of 1980 in a poll of European sports-writers by the Associated Press and United Press International. But he soon disappeared into the fog that surrounds speed skating in the United States except during an Olympic year. Not that he objected.

"I guess I shouldn't say this because I don't want to hurt anyone's feelings, but I don't like awards," he said a year later. "And I don't like to make speeches. What can someone twenty-two years old tell any-one? If I wait until I'm fifty, then I'll know what mistakes I've made."

Heiden didn't make any mistakes at Lake Placid, where his five gold medals surely helped inspire Bonnie Blair and thousands of other young speed skaters around the world. One of those thousands was Johann Olav Koss, then a twelve-year-old speed skater in Oslo, Norway.

"Johann was not a special talent for skating, but he was a special talent for training," his first coach, Svein Havard Sletten, has said, alluding to the time when Koss joined the Strommen Club at age eight. "He wanted to train very hard, very young. That is good for the

Johann Olav Koss thunders to the 1,500 gold at Lillehammer.

heart. And if he did not do well in a race, it was never my fault. It was always his fault."

Koss enjoyed training more than he enjoyed winning, because he didn't win that much until he emerged at sixteen as an age-group Norwegian national champion. In 1991 he set world records in the 5,000 and 10,000; at Albertville he won the gold in the 1,500 and a silver medal in the 10,000. But in the months before Lillehammer he doubted his skates.

"The blades are set at the wrong angle," he insisted. "I've got to get them set correctly."

Despite three trips to a skate manufacturer in Holland, the problem continued. Finally a Norwegian technician set the blades properly. Then Koss skated into the world's Olympic consciousness in Lillehammer, setting three world records while winning the 5,000, 1,500, and 10,000, in that order.

His Norwegian followers were chanting, "Jo-hann! Jo-hann! Jo-hann!" as he roared to the 5,000 gold, Norway's first in those Winter Games.

"That was the greatest moment of my life," he said later. "To feel the Norwegian people behind me, this was beyond what I can express."

Buttons shouting *Koss the Boss* appeared in Olympic shops, but Norwegians soon realized their idol was also a medical student with a sense of humanity; his parents, Arne and Sofia, are doctors. After winning the 1,500, he announced that he was donating his bonus money from equipment sponsors and the Norwegian Olympic Committee (225,000 kroner, or about $30,000) to Lillehammer Olympic Aid, organized in 1992 to provide relief to the victims of the civil war in the former Yugoslavia who were living in Sarajevo, the Winter Games site a decade earlier. By 1994 the program had expanded to helping children in other war-torn countries in Africa, Asia, the Middle East, and Latin America.

"I will have work when I finish medical school," he said, alluding to the money he was donating. "Norway needs doctors."

He also asked every Norwegian to donate 10 kroner ($1.37) to Olympic Aid for every Norwegian gold medal. As an Olympic Aid ambassador six months earlier Koss had visited Eritrea, on Africa's northeastern coast, where children were playing on burned-out tanks. Three months after the Winter Games in Lillehammer he returned to Eritrea on an Olympic Aid flight with tons of sporting goods and supplies.

"Sometimes the poorest people," he has said, "have the richest spirit."

Few athletes have displayed as rich a spirit as Koss has. He emerged as a representative to the United Nations Children's Fund, and he campaigned for Olympic Truce, a movement led by the IOC to produce a cessation of armed conflict throughout the world during the sixteen days of the 1996 Summer Games in Atlanta. He organized the JOK Run in Kristiansand, about 150 miles from Oslo, in which the disabled and able-bodied run together.

In the Olympic connection, Koss was inspired by Eric Heiden's five gold medals. So was Dan Jansen, whose saga inspired thousands of others.

Dan Jansen's Drama

On Valentine's Day 1988 in the Olympic Village in Calgary, Canada, twenty-two-year-old Dan, the youngest of the nine Jansen children, was awakened by a telephone call. His sister, Jane Beres, the twenty-seven-year-old mother of three little girls, had died of leukemia five hours after he had spoken to her for what would be the last time. She had been ill for more than a year.

"She could understand me, but she couldn't talk back to me," he recalled. "She did understand what I said, and I'm very happy about that."

Even before his sister's death the square-jawed Jansen had planned on remaining in Calgary to skate because "that's what Jane would've wanted." Now he had to skate that night in the 500-meter race. After having won two 500 races in the world sprint championships in West Allis a week earlier, he was the favorite for the gold medal. At the gun he got off to a slower start than usual, and on the first turn he fell. The white smear across the ice to the padded gray wall that his body made resembled the skid marks of an automobile accident.

"I wasn't gripping the ice real well," he said later. "I had that problem in the warm-ups. I felt I could not push as hard as I wanted."

Four nights later, striding down the straightaway in the 1,000, Jansen fell again. Speed skaters occasionally fall on a turn but seldom on a straightaway. The falls haunted him. About a year before the 1992 Winter Games in Albertville, he decided to consult Jim Loehr, a sports psychologist in Saddlebrook, Florida.

"The way I interpreted it," Loehr later explained, "Dan's fall in Calgary was the greatest gift he could give his sister. Unconsciously he did not want to experience the happiest moment of his life at the same time and on the same day that his sister, whom he cherished more than anyone in his family, had died."

But at Albertville Jansen, now twenty-six years old, finished fourth in the 500 and twenty-sixth in the 1,000.

With the rescheduled two-year gap between the Winter Games, he soon had another chance at Lillehammer in 1994, but in the 500 he slipped, touched the ice momentarily, and finished eighth. Only the 1,000 remained. In earlier years he had disliked the 1,000, but Loehr had him write every night for two years, "I love the 1,000. I love the 1,000. I love the 1,000." Before arriving at Lillehammer, he had won five of his eight 1,000-meter races. He also was leading the World Cup standings in that event.

"You can't get too strong," his coach, Peter Mueller, often told him. "And you can't have too much endurance."

To develop his strength and endurance, Jansen often ran eight to twelve miles. His skating workouts consisted of thirty minutes non-stop: four laps hard, two laps easy, hard turns, easy turns. After that he ran or duckwalked up a steep ski hill three or four times and finished with a forty-five-minute run. All the while he was thinking about how he could improve his technique.

"I relish the challenge," he writes in his autobiography, *Full Circle*, "of making subtle adjustments that cut a couple hundredths off my time."

The morning of the Olympic 1,000 in Lillehammer, Jansen arrived at the Viking Ship Oval three hours before his race. He jogged, jumped around, and stretched for forty-five minutes. On the ice he glided a few slow laps, did some accelerations and starts, then checked the sharpness of his skate blades.

Six years after his two falls in Calgary, he not only won the Olympic gold medal in the 1,000 but set a world record.

Dan Jansen glows with his daughter, Jane, at Lillehammer.

During the decade of his disappointments, millions of Americans were aware of Jansen's saga. When he finally won his Olympic gold medal, America smiled. President Clinton phoned him from the White House, and Hillary Rodham Clinton, the First Lady, phoned him from a jet taking her to Wisconsin.

"Finally," he said later, "I feel like I've made other people happy instead of having them feel sorry for me."

Seldom had an athlete's story touched the nation as Dan Jansen's had. Skating his victory lap, he held his nine-month-old daughter, Jane, named in memory of his late sister.

"We wanted to end it this way," his wife, Robin, said. "With the new Jane in our lives."

That night Dan Jansen stood on the Olympic platform, his gold medal around his neck, his arms raised with a bouquet of roses in his right hand, a smile of fulfillment on his face. When "The Star-Spangled Banner" was played, he saluted. Asked later whom he was saluting, he smiled.

"To Jane," he said.

When a Medal Is a Medal

JEFF BLATNICK WAS ENTERING THE ARENA FOR THE gold-medal final in Greco-Roman wrestling's super heavyweight division at the 1984 Summer Games when he heard his mother call, "Do it for Dave."

Of all the Olympic sports, Greco-Roman wrestling is one of the few that are virtually the same as they were in the original Olympics. Unlike freestyle wrestlers, Greco-Roman wrestlers may use only their arms, not their legs; they cannot hold opponents below the waist. Blatnick's opponent was Thomas Johansson of Sweden, but he had endured other opponents.

Jeff Blatnick pins the Greco-Roman gold at Los Angeles.

Seven years earlier his older brother, Dave, had died in a motorcycle accident; two years earlier he had needed surgery and radiation treatments to cure Hodgkin's disease.

Now, after having won the gold medal, the 248-pound six-four Olympian from Niskayuna, New York, dropped to his knees, crossed himself, and clasped his hands in prayer. Soon he was on his feet, gasping for breath and sobbing as he started to thank his family and friends. Suddenly he stopped.

"I'm sorry," he said. "I can't talk now."

He didn't need to talk. His tears had explained everything. And with television bringing those tears into homes all over America, he touched the nation's heart as few Olympians have.

"I'm embarrassed, but I'm not ashamed," he said later. "I guess it's like people always say, 'The big guys are babies.'"

Hardly. Originally a freestyle wrestler at Springfield (Massachusetts) College, where he earned a physical education degree, he might have earned a gold medal at Moscow if not for the 1980 boycott. The next year he noticed lumps along the right side of his neck. He was diagnosed as having Hodgkin's disease, a form of cancer.

"The cure rate for what I had was ninety-five percent," he recalled. "I was lucky enough to be in that ninety-five percent."

Wherever the twenty-seven-year-old wrestler went after his Olympic victory, he was surrounded by autograph seekers. One, an older man, mentioned that he was about to enter the hospital for an operation.

"What you've done," the man said, "is very encouraging."

"Just keep a good frame of mind," the gold medalist said.

Jeff Blatnick's inspiring scenario at Los Angeles emerged from one of the Olympics' least publicized sports. Not many people knew what Greco-Roman wrestling was all about, but they knew it was the Olympics, and that was enough. It's like that with many of the other sports that always seem to be in the shadows of the more popular Olympic sports. Every four years, another sport or two is usually added, often after having been what is called a demonstration sport.

Baseball, for example, was a demonstration sport in eight different Summer Games (from 1904 to 1988) until it was recognized in 1992 as a medal sport.

But in every official Olympic sport, no matter how popular or obscure, a medal is a medal, especially a gold medal.

Pat Spurgin was eleven years old when she told her shooting coach, Ralph Saunders, about her ambition to win an Olympic medal. And in 1984 at Los Angeles, when she was eighteen, during the air rifle competition she took a deep breath.

"I told myself," she said later, " 'Pat, you've gone this far, don't lose it now.' "

In her last five shots Spurgin scored four 10s and one 9 to win a gold medal.

Darrell Pace's Tour

Even before those 1984 Summer Games began, Darrell Pace was counting on another archery medal to go with the gold he had earned in Montreal. Alerted that if he were to win a medal in Los Angeles, he would be invited to join a tour of American medal winners, he turned to his wife, Beth.

"Block those days out," he said. "I'm sure we'll be going on that tour."

True to his prediction, Pace won another gold. Sometimes that gold can be contagious. When Steve Hegg was a teenager, he beat skier Billy Johnson, whose gold medal in the 1984 men's downhill inspired Hegg, now a cyclist, five months later at Los Angeles.

"I thought," Hegg said, "Billy's got his gold medal, now I want mine."

Hegg got his gold in cycling's 4,000-meter individual pursuit. He had taken up cycling to stay in shape for skiing, but realizing that he couldn't do justice to both sports, he concentrated on cycling.

"The way the seasons run together," he said, "you would need sixteen months in every year."

Time is the enemy of all aspiring Olympic athletes: time to develop their talent, time to train properly, time to gear themselves to being at their best on the day they compete for an Olympic medal. Not the day before, not the day after, but that one day. Perhaps no athlete needs to do that more than a weight lifter, as Vassily Alexeyev knew better than anybody.

In addition to being the 1972 and 1976 gold medalist, this black-haired barrel-chested 324-pound super-heavyweight set eighty-two world records while winning eight consecutive world championships.

His lifestyle symbolized the essence of the Soviet sports culture. He lived in a brick bungalow in Shakhty, about eight hundred miles southwest of Moscow, with his wife, Olympiada, and their two sons. He was paid five hundred rubles a month (then worth about seven hundred dollars), ostensibly for being a mining engineer. Since his monthly rent was only twelve rubles, he had a pleasant lifestyle: working out, competing, and tending to his garden, where he grew strawberries, peppers, and roses. Throughout the Soviet Union and the world he was known primarily for having been the first man to lift five hundred pounds.

Time also betrayed rower Anita DeFrantz. After earning a bronze medal at Montreal in the women's eight-oared crew, she was deprived of a gold-medal opportunity in the pairs at Moscow by the 1980 boycott, which involved a cutback in grain sales to the Soviets.

"We want to compete," DeFrantz, a twenty-seven-year-old lawyer, complained at the time. "They can give the farmers another market for their grain, but they can't give us anything but the Olympic Games."

In the shadow sports there is usually no hope of someday earning a livelihood as a professional or of obtaining endorsement contracts. To most of these athletes that doesn't make any difference. As Jon Lugbill, a white-water canoeist on the 1992 Olympic team, said, "I didn't get into canoeing to get rich and famous. I got into it because I like it."

Greg Barton paddled a kayak for that reason and another. He was born with clubfeet that even surgery didn't help.

"My feet ended up a lot worse," he said. "After the operation, one leg was shorter than the other."

At Seoul in 1988 that didn't prevent Barton and Norm Bellingham from teaming to win the K-2 1,000-meter event in kayaking, one of the many sports that suddenly emerge during Olympic years. Bobsledding is another. In the United States the only Olympic bobsled runs are the two icy chutes built for the 1932 Winter Games on Mount Van Hoevenberg in Lake Placid, New York.

The Bobsled Sensation

In the years before bobsledding was popular in Europe, those two runs at Lake Placid enabled husky thrill seekers from the area to dominate the Winter Games until Olympic teams emerged from East Germany, Italy, Switzerland, and the Soviet Union.

"There's really no sensation in any sport compared to bobsledding," Jim Hickey once said. "I used to drive stock cars. I've ridden roller coasters. Nothing gives you the same thrill, the same sense of adventure."

From 1964 to 1984 at least one of the Hickey brothers (Jim, Bob, and Bill) was on the U.S. Olympic bobsled team. And since 1964 another form of sledding, the luge, has added to the appeal of the Winter Games.

"Having to go straight as an arrow down the straightaway," says Frank Masley, a three-time Olympian and ten-time American champion, "knowing that you have to be very subtle with every move, it's a thrill."

That thrill transcends every Olympic sport, whether it be table tennis or badminton, yachting or team handball, field hockey or judo.

Unlike a relatively modern game like baseball, many Olympic sports have evolved for centuries. Take fencing. When the twelve-time U.S. saber champion, Peter Westbrook, was a youngster, he often

Mount Van Hoevenberg bobsled run at Lake Placid

watched *Zorro* on television. One day, at age ten, he carved a Z in his mother's coffee table.

"My mother's brand-new table," he said. "Luckily she didn't spank me the way she should have. Very understanding mother. Very understanding."

Westbrook earned a rare fencing scholarship to New York University, one of the few colleges to sponsor a fencing team. His coach there, Csaba Elthes, who was also the Olympic coach, polished him into a bronze medalist at Los Angeles in 1984.

Another sport that has been around for centuries is horseback riding, known officially as equestrian.

The best rider in American history, Bill Steinkraus, won Olympic medals over a twenty-year span: a team bronze in 1952, a team silver in 1960, an individual gold in show jumping on a horse named Snowbound in 1968 at Mexico City, and a team silver in show jumping in 1972.

Fencing and show jumping are two of the five events in what is known as the modern pentathlon, an Olympic sport dating back to the time of military couriers. The other three are a 300-meter freestyle swim, a .22-caliber pistol shooting, and a 4,000-meter cross-country run.

Some sports, such as volleyball, have expanded in world popularity primarily because of the Olympics, but they're still growing.

Karch Kiraly, the son of a Hungarian refugee physician, led UCLA to three national college volleyball titles, but the game was considered a California beach pastime until he lifted the U.S. team to a gold medal in 1984 and again in 1988. With its players diving, leaping, and smashing a ball slightly smaller than a basketball over a thirty-two-foot net nearly eight feet above the floor, volleyball is a spectacle. But despite the American men's two gold medals, volleyball is still in the Olympic shadows.

"It won't have arrived," Paul Sunderland, a member of the 1984 team, said, "until the people who see us in an airport stop asking us what basketball team we play for."

Karch Kiraly spikes his Korean volleyball opponents.

IN EVERY OLYMPIC STADIUM THERE IS ALWAYS THE LONELY runner. Usually from a small nation, the lonely runner is a lap or two behind the winner in a distance race, but the lonely runner plods on, determined to finish. When the huge crowd notices the lonely runner, the cheer begins. But it's not a mocking cheer. It's a rooting cheer that seems to lift the lonely runner around the track. And when the lonely runner finally crosses the finish line, an even louder cheer erupts.

The lonely runner has triumphed. Not won a gold medal but triumphed. The lonely runner has completed an Olympic race. The lonely runner has participated.

More than any other Olympic athlete, the lonely runner symbolizes why the Olympics are so popular. Because that lonely runner could be anybody in the world.

In the dazzle of its hundredth anniversary celebration, the modern Olympics are now the world's most popular sports spectacle because they are truly a world event. When the 1996 Summer Games are bounced off satellites to television screens almost everywhere in the world, that worldwide stage is the essence of why the Olympics are so popular.

Virtually every nation has an Olympic team. Whether that team consists of two or two hundred athletes, people in virtually every nation are interested in how those athletes perform.

No matter what the nation, an athlete doesn't have to win a gold medal or a silver medal or a bronze medal. Just being in the Olympics is enough. Going there. Marching with your team in the opening ceremonies. Competing in your event. Returning home with the memory.

Representing a big nation or a small nation, you will always be an Olympian. If you win or if you finish last, you will always be an Olympian.

Yes, soccer's World Cup is popular worldwide. So are basketball, boxing, golf, tennis, and track and field. In the United States football and baseball rival basketball's popularity, and ice hockey's popularity is growing. But because the Olympics involve so many sports, it's more popular than any one sport ever could be.

So many sports produce so many stories. Sometimes those stories involve familiar names, such as Michael Jordan, Magic Johnson, and Larry Bird, who were among the members of the Dream Team, which dominated the 1992 basketball tournament in Barcelona. But those stories often produce new names, such as the virtually unknown members of the 1980 United States hockey team, which stunned the Soviet Union's steamroller.

The Olympics never go stale. They occur only once every two years on a four-year cycle. When it's time for the Olympics, they are a novelty again. The 1998 Winter Games will be held on the snowy slopes of Nagano, Japan; the 2000 Summer Games will stretch alongside the sunny harbor of Sydney, Australia; the 2002 Winter Games will be on display in the chill of Salt Lake City, Utah. And in the years that follow, the Olympics will move around the world as no other sports event does.

Politics sometimes disrupt the Olympic ideal, but in the theater of world sports the Summer Games and the Winter Games are always center stage.

Index